XML

A Quick Reference of More Than 300
XML Tasks, Terms and Tricks

FROM A TO Z

Heather A. Williamson

XML From A to Z:
A Quick Reference of More Than 300 XML Tasks, Terms and Tricks

Published by
Redmond Technology Press
8581 154th Avenue NE
Redmond, WA 98052
www.redtechpress.com

Library of Congress Catalog Card No: applied for

ISBN 1-931150-45-1

Printed and bound in the United States of America.

9 8 7 6 5 4 3 2 1

Distributed by
Independent Publishers Group
814 N. Franklin St.
Chicago, IL 60610
www.ipgbook.com

Designer: Minh-Tam S. Le
Editor: Paula Thurman

INTRODUCTION

You should find *XML From A to Z* easy to use. You only need to know that the book organizes its information—key tasks and important terms—alphabetically in order to use the book. You'll find it helpful, however, if you understand what this book assumes about your computer skills, what you should know about the XML language from the very start, and what editorial conventions this book uses. This short introduction provides this information.

What You Should Know About XML and Other Web Languages

You don't need to be computer expert to either use this book or write XML documents. Definitely not. But you want to be comfortable working with your computer, a text editor (such as Microsoft Notepad, MacWrite, or one of the many Linux text editors), and be comfortable with the concept, if not execution of, a markup language.

For example, you should know how to turn your computer on and off, how to start and stop programs, how to choose menu commands, and how to work with dialog boxes. This book doesn't provide this type of computer operation information.

If you need this information for your computer, you need to take an online tutorial for your operating system, get a friend to give you a quick lesson, or acquire another book on the operating system you are using.

TIP   *Any short book on Windows, Macintosh, or Linux machines will tell you what you need to know, but if you're a business user of Windows 2000 or Windows XP, you may want to look at the* Effective Executive's Guide to Windows 2000 *or the* Effective Executive's Guide to Windows XP. *These books supply a tutorial on Windows geared for business professionals.*

What You Should Know About XML

You don't need to know anything about XML to use this book. But because understanding the XML language will make using XML and this book easier, the following should help you.

- XML is a markup language.
- XML tags are used to define document content without formatting.
- XML is a cousin of HTML, but with a more strict structure.
- XML is a structure upon which other document markup languages are built.
- XML is constantly being expanded and modified to improve its use for distributing information.
- XML is quickly becoming the most popular format for sharing information, including e-commerce data, between businesses and consumers, businesses and businesses, and within individual corporate structures.
- XML documents must be well-formed.
- XML documents should be validated with a Schema or a DTD.
- XML documents can be viewed with all of today's most popular Web browsers, including Internet Explorer 5, Netscape Navigator 6 (requires a style sheet), and Opera 5.
- XML is a text language, and it can be created using any simple text editor, although there are many other editors available just for XML.

What You Should Know About This Book

You already know the most important feature of this book—that it organizes its task descriptions and term definitions alphabetically. But let me comment quickly on the book's other conventions.

- When this book refers to some box or button label, the label description appears in all initial capital letters. So, while the Connections tab of the Internet Options dialog box in Internet Explorer 5 includes a radio button labeled "Never dial a connection," this book would refer to the Never Dial A Connection radio button. The initial capital letters, then, signal you that the book refers to an on-screen label.
- When this book refers to XML syntax and code, the code will appear in a monospaced font such as Courier, as shown in the following example:

```
<order>

    <name type="manager"> R. Cypher </name>

    <company type="client"> Chimera Corporation
    </company>

</order>
```

- This book's pictures of windows and dialog boxes may look a bit funny to you because they use a low display resolution to make the buttons, boxes, and text look larger. Less information fits on the screen when the resolution is low, unfortunately, but what you see you can read. If the book's screen pictures had used a higher resolution, images would be very difficult to see clearly.

And that's everything you should know to get started. Good luck. Be patient in your learning. Have fun with XML, it's an amazing language. And be sure to read the Troubleshooting entry if you encounter problems.

Heather A. Williamson

heather@catsback.com

Enterprise, Oregon, October 2001

XML FROM A TO Z

<!ATTLIST>

The <!ATTLIST> declaration notifies your parser that you are working with an attribute, rather than an element or entity declaration. Attributes declarations in a DTD use the following structure:

```
<!ATTLIST element_name

    attribute_name attribute_type default_value>
```

element_name

The element_name specifies an element used in the document and declared in the DTD.

attribute_name

The attribute_name is the identifier that you use to separate this attribute from the other attributes defined for this element. Attribute names have the same restrictions that element names do: they must start with a letter and can only contain letters, numbers, underscores, and colons. The colon is reserved for providing reference to namespaces and should not be used outside of a namespace prefix setup.

attribute_type

The attribute_type is one of the following data types:
- CDATA
- ENTITY, ENTITIES
- Enumerated
- ID
- IDREF, IDREFS
- NMTOKEN, NMTOKENS
- NOTATION

default_value

The default_value is the initial value of the attribute used if the attribute is not specified with the element. Attribute values can be either an actual value, as shown in the following example, or one of the keywords: #FIXED, #IMPLIED, or #REQUIRED.

```
<!ATTLIST name

    type CDATA "billing">
```

#FIXED

When the attribute can have only one value, which is both a default and unchangeable, then you need to apply the #FIXED keyword to your <!ATTLIST> statement.

```
<!ATTLIST name

    type CDATA #FIXED "billing">
```

Authors aren't required to declare the #FIXED attribute in a document. The parser will automatically use the default value. If an author does use the #FIXED attribute in a document, then it must have the same value as the default value specified in the DTD; otherwise, an error will be generated.

#IMPLIED

This keyword allows you to include an attribute, without providing a default value or requiring that the value be supplied.

```
<!ATTLIST name CDATA #IMPLIED>
```

#REQUIRED

When your attribute doesn't have a default value, then you may need to specify that an attribute be applied to an element. By associating the #RE-QUIRED keyword to your attribute declaration, you can force the element to have that attribute in order to be validated.

```
<!ATTLIST name CDATA #REQUIRED>
```

<!ATTLIST> Declaration Example

Take the following XML element for example:

```
<name type="primary"> Richard Cypher </name>
```

This element, name, has one attribute, type, which identifies the type of contact represented by Richard Cypher. This element would be declared in the following manner within the DTD for this document:

```
<!ELEMENT name (#PCDATA)>

<!ATTLIST name type CDATA "billing">
```

The element "name" contains parsed character data (#PCDATA). The second statement identifies an attribute "type," applied to the "name" element, which contains character data, represented by CDATA in the attribute statement, with a default value of "billing".

Attribute Declaration Rules

Attribute declarations must use the following rules:

- The name of the element has to be specified within the <!ATTLIST> declaration.

- You can declare your attributes before or after your elements.

- You can declare attributes multiple times for the same element but only the first declaration of the attribute is used.

- You can declare attributes for elements that do not exist.

Applying Attribute to Multiple Elements

In many cases, the same attribute is applied to multiple elements. In this example the type attribute has been applied to two different elements and in each instance has different content:

```
<order type="web">

    <name type="billing"> Richard Cypher </name>

</order>
```

Within the DTD for this document, you would need to define both the order and name elements as well as their respective type attributes. One possible declaration is shown in the following DTD:

```
<!ELEMENT order (name+)>

    <!ATTLIST order type (web|mail|fax|phone)>

<!ELEMENT name (#PCDATA)>

    <!ATTLIST name type (billing|shipping|both)>
```

Applying Multiple Attributes to One Element

In many cases, multiple attributes are applied to a single element. In this example the type and idnum attributes have been applied to the name element:

```
<order>

    <name type="billing" idnum="99-00887"> Richard
    Cypher </name>

</order>
```

Within the DTD for this document, you would need to define both the project and name elements as well as their respective type attributes. One possible declaration is shown in the following DTD:

```
<!ELEMENT name (#PCDATA)>

<!ATTLIST name

    type (billing|shipping|both)

    idnum CDATA  #REQUIRED>
```

As you can see, each attribute for the "name" element was defined on a single line inside a single <!ATTLIST> statement.

SEE ALSO *Elements, Namespaces*

<!DOCTYPE>

The <!DOCTYPE> declaration adds a DTD to your XML document. You can use them to either link to your DTD or include an inline DTD.

Linking External DTDs

The structure of the basic <!DOCTYPE> statement to link to an external DTD is as follows:

```
<!DOCTYPE root_element_name SYSTEM "DTD_URL"]>
```

The parts of the <!DOCTYPE> statement which links to an external DTD include the following:

- **root_element_name:** The name of the root element (first element) of the XML document.
- **SYSTEM:** An XML keyword specifying that the DTD is for the current system (private), and not a public DTD such as the one defining HTML.
- **DTD_URL:** The Internet address of the DTD being used to validate the XML document.

4

NOTE   *You can link to a PUBLIC DTD, such as defines standard HTML documents by using the following format:*

```
<!DOCTYPE root_element_name PUBLIC "DTD_name"
"DTD_URL">
```

Where the PUBLIC keyword notes that the DTD being accessed is made for public dissemination, and DTD_name references the name that the original organization has given that DTD. The following statement specifies a PUBLIC DTD.

```
<!DOCTYPE orderlist PUBLIC "-//My Business//
DTD Orders//EN

"http://mybusiness.com/dtds/order.dtd">
```

The following XML document uses the <!DOCTYPE> statement to link to an external system DTD called order.dtd:

```
<?xml version="1.0" encoding="Latin-1"
standalone="yes"?>

<!DOCTYPE order SYSTEM "order.dtd">

<order>

        <name type="billing"> R. Cypher </name>

        <company type="billing"> Chimera Corporation
        </company>

 . . . .

</order>
```

The actual document type declaration appears on one line, and it specifies the file to use when validating this particular XML document. In this case, the order.dtd file validates the XML document, as shown below:

```
<!DOCTYPE order SYSTEM "order.dtd">
```

In addition to the declarative <!DOCTYPE> statement, the <order> element has been identified as the root element of the document. The SYSTEM declaration identifies this DTD as being part of a local, or nonpublic, selection of DTDs. A DTD can be referenced as either a SYSTEM or a PUBLIC document type definition. The actual name of the file is the URL, in this case a relative URL, for the actual file containing the DTD information.

Adding Inline DTDs

There are many reasons you may wish to link your DTD to your document rather than embed it within your document text. Of these many reasons, the foremost is the ability to use a single DTD with multiple documents. Not to mention the fact that it allows you to shrink the size of your XML document by the amount of space taken up with the DTD.

Of course, if you are creating a document just for yourself, and it will most likely be the only document of its particular markup, then you may wish to include the DTD within the body of the XML document.

NOTE   *You can use both an internal and external DTD together. This allows you to use the embedded DTD for those document elements that are specific to this one document and still is able to reference elements from a standard DTD from another location.*

The document type declaration changes some if you are going to actually embed the DTD code within your XML document, as you can see from the following basic syntax:

```
<!DOCTYPE root_element_name [

    Element and attribute declarations

]>
```

As you can see from the following example, the <!DOCTYPE> statement specifies the inline element declaration for the order element.

```
<?xml version="1.0" encoding="Latin-1"
standalone="yes"?>

<!DOCTYPE order [

  <!ELEMENT order ANY>

  ]>

<order>

  <name type="manager"> R. Cypher </name>

  <company type="client"> Chimera Corporation
  </company>

</order>
```

Within this XML document, three lines make up the body of this DTD. These three lines, shown in the following code, include the <!DOCTYPE statement, the order root-element designation, and the actual code of the DTD. When placing your DTD code within your XML document, you must

6

wrap the DTD text within square brackets, shown here at the end of the first line and the start of the third line. These brackets allow the parser to identify the start and stop of the DTD declarations separate from the remaining XML code and the default <!DOCTYPE> statement construction.

```
<!DOCTYPE order [

  <!ELEMENT order ANY>

]>
```

SEE ALSO *<!ATTLIST>, <!ELEMENT>, Attributes, DTD, Elements*

<!ELEMENT>

A DTD is composed of individual element and attribute type declarations. Each element declaration is identified with the following basic syntax:

```
<!ELEMENT element_name content>
```

element_name

This is the name of the element, for example order, name, or company.

content

Each element has a set of allowable content. The DTD identifies the type of content used with any particular element. Your options include "EMPTY", "ANY", *mixed content*, or *children.*

EMPTY

Specifies that this element contain no content, although it can have attributes.

```
<!ELEMENT order EMPTY>
```

ANY

Specifies that this element can contain any content whether that content is text, child elements, or a combination of both

```
<!ELEMENT order ANY>
```

Mixed Content

Allows you to specify the exact content you wish the element to contain. You can specify only text data (#PCDATA) or a combination of text and specified child elements.

```
<!ELEMENT order (name | company | #PCDATA)>
```

Children

Specifies child element(s) found within the body of the identified element. This content can't contain any character data.

```
<!ELEMENT address (street, suite, city, state, zip,
phone)>
```

SEE ALSO *Content Type*

<!ELEMENT> Declaration Example

In addition to defining the elements used in the document, the DTD must define the various entities, attributes, and notations used and how these all work together with the elements themselves. Use the following XML document showing two order listings as an example:

```
<orderlist>

  <order>

    <name>R. Cypher</name>

    <company> Chimera Corp. </company>

    <address> 19 Driveby Ln., Alder, OR 99999
    </address>

    <total> $21.49 </total>

  </order>

  <order>

    <name>K. Wizard</name>

    <company> Tualatin Paper </company>

    <address> 88 Mulberry Ln., Tualatin, WA, 99999
    </address>

    <total> $65.89 </total>

  </order>

</orderlist>
```

In this example, you have a primary element called orderlist that serves as the root element for your document. Define this element before any others in your DTD. The element declaration statement for orderlist would be

```
<!ELEMENT orderlist (order*)>
```

This declaration of the element orderlist states that this element can only contain child elements with the name order. The asterisk (*) by the name order specifies that the element can occur within orderlist zero or more times.

The declaration statement for the <order> element would appear as

```
<!ELEMENT order (name, company, address, total)>
```

In this case, the element <order> can only contain a series of elements listed as <name>, <company>, <address>, and <total>. You must also define each of these elements:

```
<!ELEMENT name (#PCDATA)>

<!ELEMENT company (#PCDATA)>

<!ELEMENT address (#PCDATA)>

<!ELEMENT total (#PCDATA)>
```

The definition of these elements specifies that they can contain character data (#PCDATA) but no child elements. When placed altogether within our XML document, we have a single document that can be transported anywhere in its entirety and not lose any ability to be validated.

```
<?xml version="1.0" standalone="yes"?>

<!DOCTYPE orderlist [

<!ELEMENT orderlist (order*)>

<!ELEMENT order (name, company, address, total)>

<!ELEMENT name (#PCDATA)>

<!ELEMENT company (#PCDATA)>

<!ELEMENT address(#PCDATA)>

<!ELEMENT total (#PCDATA)>

 ]>

<orderlist>

  <order>

    <name>R. Cypher</name>

    <company> Chimera Corp. </company>

    <address> 19 Driveby Ln., Alder, OR 99999
    </address>
```

```
<total> $21.49 </total>

</order>

<order>

<name>K. Wizard</name>

<company> Tualatin Paper </company>

<address> 88 Mulberry Ln., Tualatin, WA, 99999
</address>

<total> $65.89 </total>

</order>

</orderlist>
```

Element Declaration Rules

Element declarations, like anything else, have a set of rules to follow when creating your DTD:

- Declare all elements in the document.
- Element names are case sensitive making the elements ORDER and order separate elements.
- Elements declared as EMPTY can have attributes, but no content.

#PCDATA see Data Types

@IMPORT

In a Cascading Style Sheet, this rule adds an external style sheet to the document. For instance, you can assign a style sheet to your main XML document using <?xml-stylesheet?> and from within that style sheet use the @import rule to add additional style information. By having the ability to store style sheets in a series of parts, you can create a series of small style sheets that can be merged for larger, more complex documents, while using concise style sheets for smaller single-application documents.

The @import rule has the following syntax:

```
@import url(address);
```

For instance, if you were to have an XML document tracking the complete order history of a customer, you could have a series of style sheets for each portion of that document: postyles.css for purchase order data, contactstyles.css for contact data, and itemstyles.css for item data. To use all

10

of these style sheets on one XML document, you would use the following @import rules, shown first as absolute addresses and then as relative addresses:

Absolute Addresses

```
@import url(http://mybusiness.com/styles/
postyles.css);

@import url(http://mybusiness.com/styles/
contactstyles.css);

@import url(http://mybusiness.com/styles/
itemstyles.css);
```

Relative Addresses

```
@import url(/styles/postyles.css);

@import url(/styles/contactstyles.css);

@import url(/styles/itemstyles.css);
```

SEE ALSO *<?xml-stylesheet?>, Cascading Style Sheets, Style Sheets*

<?xml?>

The XML declaration must be the first line of any XML document. This statement identifies the specific version of XML used, the standalone (requiring no other documents) status of the document, and the language used to encode it. The default form of an XML declaration is

```
<?xml version="1.0" standalone="yes" encoding="UTF-
8"?>
```

Version

The version attribute of the <?xml?> declaration provides the XML browser with information about the version of the XML specification that has been followed in the development of this current document. The current version of the XML standard is 1.0, which was designated a full specification in February 1998. October 2000 saw the second edition of this specification completed.

Standalone

The standalone attribute of the <?xml?> declaration informs the XML browser of the status of the current document. If standalone="yes", then the browser will know that there are no other documents, including DTDs, style sheets, images, or stored external entities, that need to be loaded to

11

properly display the XML document. If any other document must be used to properly display and validate the document, then the standalone attribute must be set to "no."

NOTE   *All current Web browsers will properly display documents with the standalone attribute set to "no." In this case, you may wish to set your standalone attribute to "yes" even though it is a validation error. This should be done only if you know that not all users of your document will have browsers supporting the standalone="no" value.*

Encoding

The encoding attribute of the <?xml?> declaration provides the browser with information about the character encoding that is being used in the document. For instance, if you were to specify encoding="US-ASCII", then the browser would know that only English language characters were used in the document.

Basic XML Document Example

The most basic XML document includes the XML declaration statement and a root element, as shown in the following example:

```
<?xml version=1.0" standalone="yes" encoding="UTF-8">

<document>

   My Document Contents

</document>
```

SEE ALSO *Character Encoding, Character Set, XML Declaration*

<?xml-stylesheet?>

The xml-stylesheet processing instruction provides a direct link to a style sheet, of any language, used to format the current document. This style sheet can be CSS, XSL, or even DSSSL. The basic structure of the xml-stylesheet processing instruction is

```
<?xml-stylesheet type="MIME_type"
href="stylesheet_URL"?>
```

NOTE   *If you are associating a style sheet with your XML document, the value of your XML declaration's standalone attribute should be "no."*

A

type

The type attribute specifies the MIME type of the style sheet that you wish to apply to your document. The following table lists the common style-sheet MIME types.

STYLE SHEET TYPE	MIME TYPE
CSS	text/css
XSL	text/xsl
DSSSL	text/dsssl

href

The href attribute contains either the absolute or the relative URL of the style sheet document. If the address is absolute, then provide the full URI as shown in the following example:

```
<?xml-stylesheet type="text/css" href="http://
mybusiness.com/styles/orders.css"?>
```

A relative URL would have the following format:

```
<?xml-stylesheet type="text/css" href="/styles/
orders.css"?>
```

Basic Style Sheet Example

A basic XML document with an associated style sheet will appear similar to the following:

```
<?xml version="1.0" standalone="no" encoding="UTF-
8"?>

<?xml-stylesheet type="text/css" href="/styles/
orders.css"?>

<orders>

   My First Order

</orders>
```

SEE ALSO *CSS, MIME, URL, XSL*

Ancestor

XML document structure derives from the concept of a tree structure. In this system, an ancestor is an element that precedes the current element in the document tree. In the following example document, the order element is an ancestor of the itemname element.

13

```
<?xml version="1.0" standalone="yes" encoding="UTF-
8"?>

<order>

   <name> R. Cypher </name>

   <items>

      <itemname> Legal Pads - 10 Pack </itemname>

      <itemvalue> 6.99 </itemvalue>

   </items>

</order>
```

As you can see in Figure A-1, the similarity of the XML document tree to a standard genealogical tree makes the identification of ancestors quite simple.

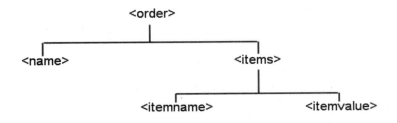

Figure A-1   XML document tree structure.

SEE ALSO *Node, Parent Elements, Tree Structures*

ANSI

The American National Standards Institute (ANSI), a nonprofit U.S.-based organization founded in 1918, is just one of the standards organizations that participate in and support the use of standards on the Internet. ANSI standards have been affecting the use of computer-based technology for the last 30 years, and continue to develop standards that affect our use of technology today. The Windows ANSI character set, used by almost all Windows users, is just one of the many character sets available for use in XML documents. For more information on ANSI, see their Web site at *http:// www.ansi.org.*

SEE ALSO *ASCII, Character Set, Unicode*

Applications see XML Applications
ASCII

The American Standard Code for Information Interchange (ASCII) is the basic language representing the 256 characters used by most computer operating systems for displaying the basic 128 printable characters and control characters, such as enter, space, and line break. Most ASCII characters are represented by character entities or can be typed from your keyboard within your XML document. You can read more about the workings of ASCII code, as well as many others, at *http://www.diffuse.org/chars.html*.

SEE ALSO *ANSI, Character Encoding, Character Set, Entities, Unicode*

Attributes

While elements define specific types of content, attributes provide more information about the data content of a specific element. Attributes are typically pieces of information such as the line item number in an order form, the color specification for a specific product ordered, or even the customer ID number of the company ordering a product.

Because attributes simply provide auxiliary or explanatory information about the contents of an element, or an element itself, there is no need to create a full statement for them. You embed them within the start tag of the element itself, as shown in the following example:

```
<order order_num="09876"> </order>
```

When you read this document, you see that the order, which could be any collection of materials or services, is associated with an order number 09876 as noted by the order_num attribute with a value, enclosed with quotation marks, of "09876".

NOTE   *In an XML document, all attribute values must be included within quotation marks. HTML did not have this requirement.*

XML has no built-in display attributes, but you can create attributes, in addition to using the Document Object Model (DOM), a scripting language such as JavaScript, and Cascading Style Sheets (CSS) or the Extensible Stylesheet Language (XSL) to create completely formatted documents such as you see every day on the Web that are based on HTML.

Attribute Types

Attributes can be any of the following data types:

- CDATA
- ENTITY, ENTITIES
- Enumerated
- ID
- IDREF, IDREFS
- NMTOKEN, NMTOKENS
- NOTATION

Attribute Rules

Attributes can have a variety of values based upon their attribute type. For instance, CDATA type attributes hold all basic text strings. However, no matter what type of attribute you are working with, the values must follow these rules:

- All attribute values must be included in quotation marks.
- All attribute values must coincide with the attribute's declared attribute type.
- All attributes, not specified for an element, will be given a default value, when the DTD or schema specifies a default value.
- All attributes are added to the opening tag of elements, including empty elements.
- Attribute names are case sensitive, and must be declared in the DTD or Schema using the same case.
- Attribute values, in the case of IDREF, IDREFS, NMTOKEN, and NMTOKENS attribute types, are case sensitive.

Attribute Declarations

Attributes are declared in a DTD by using the <!ATTLIST> statement shown in the following example:

```
<!ATTLIST element_name

    attribute_name attribute_type default_value>
```

If you opt to use an XML Schema to validate your documents, then attributes are defined there using the following notation:

```
<xsd:attribute name="attribute_name"
type="attribute_type"/>
```

SEE ALSO *<!ATTLIST>, Data Types, Schemas*

Authoring Tools

Although XML is a text-based language and you can use any text editor to create your XML documents, there are also a variety of other editors that allow you to create your XML document, Schema, or DTD and validate your document in one program.

Code Editors

The following code editors allow you to create an XML document, but do not provide any document validation services.

XML Notepad

Microsoft's XML Notepad, shown in Figure A-2, is a simple application for building and editing small XML-data-based documents. In addition to its document source view, it includes an icon-based tree view of the document showing all the document's text, attributes, comments, and child elements.

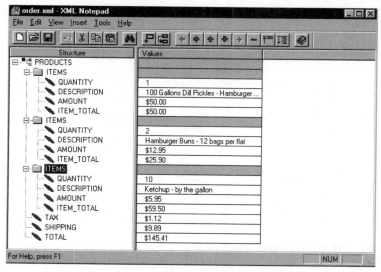

Figure A-2   Microsoft's XML Notepad.

Microsoft

msdn.microsoft.com/library/default.asp?url=/library/en-us/dnxml/html/ xmlpaddownload.asp

Available for Win95/98/NT and 2000.

XED

XED, provided by the Language Technology Group at the University of
Edinburgh, has been designed for technical users who want to hand-edit
XML documents. Its advanced keyboarding features help savvy users speed
up input, while enforcing document well-formedness.

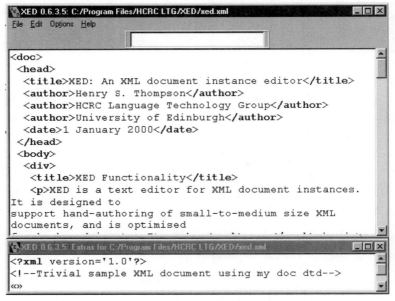

Figure A-3   XED is an advanced text editor for XML data.

Language Technology Group

www.ltg.ed.ac.uk/~ht/xed.html

Available for Win 95, 98, NT, Solaris 2.5, Linux, and FreeBSD.

Validating Editors

The following validating editors allow you to create your XML document,
your Schema, or DTD and validate your information.

XMetaL

XMetaL, developed by SoftQuad Software and shown in Figure A-4, allows you to create XML documents based upon DTDs. Within the XMetaL interface, you can see three different views of your document, including the plain text XML code view, a formatted document with element markers showing as icons, and a formatted document, as if you were viewing it through your browser. You can use your own CSS-based style sheets to control your document formatting.

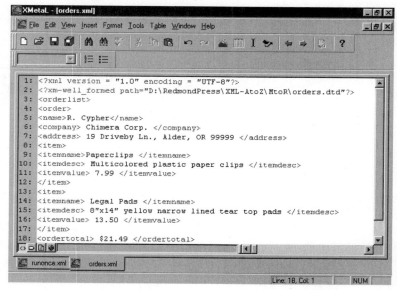

Figure A-4   XMetaL works with your other installed software to create a complete XML information management system.

SoftQuad Software

www.xmetal.com

Available for Windows 95/98/NT/2000.

Turbo XML

Tibco Extensibility's Turbo XML, shown in Figure A-5, is a completely integrated development environment created for the sole purpose of developing and managing XML documents. It includes tools to create, validate, convert, and manage your XML Schemas, documents, and DTDs.

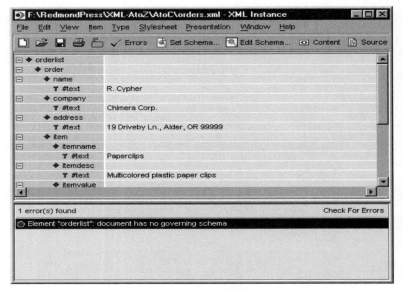

Figure A-5   Turbo XML is a completely integrated XML development environment.

Tibco Extensibility

www.extensibility.com

Available for Windows 95/98/2000 and NT, Mac OS X, Linux x86, Solaris SPARC, Solaris x86, HP-UX 11.0 and 11i, and other UNIX platforms.

XML Spy

Icon Information Systems XML Spy, shown in Figure A-6, is a complete editing environment for XML providing access to a validating text editor, a tree-based document view, a colored syntax text view, and an integrated browser that shows both CSS and XSL style sheets applied to your XML document. You can even create your XML Schemas and XSL style sheets using XML Spy.

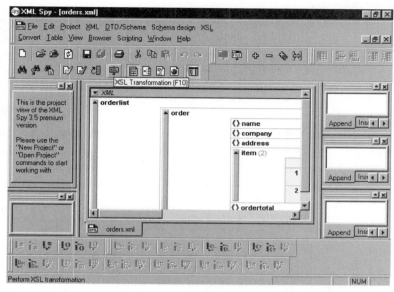

Figure A-6 XML Spy works with all XML documents including XSL style sheets and schemas.

Icon Information Systems

www.xmlspy.com

Available for Windows 95/95/2000 and NT.

Boolean Logic

Boolean logic finds values within your XML documents using XSLT, SQL statements, and other data manipulation techniques that meet a set of specified requirements.

Boolean logic uses the principles of logical comparisons between two or more items, matching them in a logical way based upon the specified operator, to collect a set of data. Take the following case as an example. Assume there is a group of people in a room that meet the descriptions listed in the following table. The examples shown in the AND, OR, and NOT sections use the data in this table in their examples.

ID	HAIR	EYES	SEX
Fred	blond	blue	male
Joe	gray	brown	male
Charlie	brown	brown	male
Sue	blond	blue	female
Alex	brown	brown	female
Leah	red	green	female

TIP   *All Search engines on the Internet use Boolean logic to find and display the results you are looking for. In most cases, typing a statement such as "XML Schemas" will be an OR operation finding all documents showing instances of the words "XML" and "Schemas." You can specify that you need both words in your search results by using "XML AND Schemas."*

AND Operator (&)

The AND (&) operator assumes that all of the listed requirements in a statement are true, as shown in Figure B-1.

A	B	C
0	0	0
0	1	0
1	0	0
1	1	1

Figure B-1   If A and B are both 1, then C must also be 1.

Using our list of people, the following statement would use the Boolean operator AND to find Fred individually out of the group of people.

```
(Hair="blond") AND (Sex="male")
```

Assume for a moment the following statement:

```
Hair="blond"
```

With this statement both Fred and Sue would have been returned as true values because both of these individuals have blond hair. If the statement would have been

```
Sex="male"
```

22

Then Fred, Joe, and Charlie would have been returned as true values, as they are all male individuals in our test data. In order to find Fred specifically, you have to compare at least two identifying characteristics of the answer set, as shown in the following table.

HAIR="BLOND"	SEX="MALE"
Fred	Fred
Sue	Joe
	Charlie

The only individual who meets both characteristics is Fred.

OR Operator (|)

The OR (|) operator assumes that the statement is true, if either of the requirements in the statement is true, as shown in Figure B-1.

A	B	C
0	0	0
0	1	1
1	0	1
1	1	1

Figure B-2   If A is 1 OR B is 1 (or both), then C is 1.

Using the list of people in the previous table, the following statement would use the Boolean operator OR to find all of the people who are either blond haired or male in the group of people.

```
(Hair="blond") OR (Sex="male")
```

Assume for a moment the following statement:

```
Hair="blond"
```

With this statement both Fred and Sue would have been returned as true values because both of these individuals have blond hair. When the statement is

```
Sex="male"
```

Then Fred, Joe, and Charlie are returned as true values, as they are all male individuals in our test data. Because the OR statement asks that only one of the specified statements is true, then Fred, Joe, Charlie, and Sue would all be answers to the question.

NOT Operator

The NOT operator is an inverter. It takes a statement as input and produces as output its opposite. Figure B-3 shows a logic table for the NOT operator.

A	C
0	1
1	0

Figure B-3   If A is 1, C is 0. C is always the opposite of A.

Assuming our list of people, the following statement would use the Boolean operator NOT to find all of the people who do not have blond hair in the group.

```
NOT(Hair="blond")
```

With this statement everyone but Fred and Sue would have been returned as true values because these are the only individuals with blond hair. When the statement is

```
NOT(Sex="male")
```

Then Sue, Alex, and Leah are returned as true values, as they are all female individuals in our test data.

NAND Operator

NAND is the combination of NOT and AND. Figure B-4 shows the logic functions of this operator.

A	B	C
0	0	1
0	1	1
1	0	1
1	1	0

Figure B-4   If A and B are both 1, then C is 0, while in all other combinations C is 1.

Using our test group, the following statement would use the Boolean operator NAND to find everyone except Fred.

```
(Hair="blond") NAND (Sex="male")
```

Assume for a moment the following statement:

```
Hair="blond"
```

24

With this statement both Fred and Sue would have been returned as true values because both of these individuals have blond hair. If the statement would have been

```
Sex="male"
```

Then Fred, Joe, and Charlie would have been returned as true values, as they are all male individuals in our test data. In order to eliminate Fred specifically, you have to compare at least two identifying characteristics of the answer set, as shown in the following table.

HAIR="BLOND"	SEX="MALE"	EVERONE ELSE
Fred	Fred	Alex
Sue	Joe	Leah
	Charlie	

The only individual that meets both characteristics is Fred. Because the NAND operator says that the result set can't meet both of these requirements, but may meet one of them, our resulting answer would be everyone but Fred: Sue, Joe, Charlie, Alex, and Leah.

NOR Operator

The NOR operator inverts the work of the OR operator. Where OR allows either one or the other of the statements to be true, to evaluate to true, NOR specifies that if either of the values are true, then they are not in the result set. Figure B-5 shows the logic structure of the NOR operator.

A	B	C
0	0	1
0	1	0
1	0	0
1	1	0

Figure B-5   Only if A and B are 0 will C be 1.

Using our study group, the following statement would use the Boolean operator NOR to find all of the people who are neither blond haired nor male in the group of people.

```
(Hair="blond") NOR (Sex="male")
```

Assume for a moment the following statement:

```
Hair="blond"
```

With this statement both Fred and Sue would have been returned as true values because both of these individuals have blond hair. When the statement is

```
Sex="male"
```

then Fred, Joe, and Charlie are returned as true values, as they are all male individuals in our test data. Because the NOR statement asks that neither of the specified statements is true for the result group, then only Alex and Leah would be returned in answer to the query.

SEE ALSO *Database, SQL*

Canonical XML

The Canonical XML working draft focuses on creating subsets of the elements used in an existing XML document, to use as a basis for comparisons to other similar documents. If you were to do a byte-by-byte comparison of two XML documents, even using the same markup they would appear completely different to the computer because of the data content of each. Canonical XML attempts to overcome this difficulty, which makes it hard for companies to compare and work with similar documents from different departments because of the order of the elements and the varying data that they contain. By creating a subset of elements used in the document, without including content, then the computer can more accurately compare two document instances and come up with meaningful data. You can find out more about Canonical XML's development at the World Wide Web Consortium's Web site located at *http://www.w3.org/Signature/*.

SEE ALSO *Digital Signatures, World Wide Web Consortium, XML*

Cascading Style Sheets

Cascading Style Sheets (CSS) enable document authors and users to control the presentation of document information. CSS separates the presentation elements of a document from its content, providing the formatting of information for XML documents. CSS allows you to tailor the display of your document for visual applications, aural devices, print, Braille, TTY machines, or even the television. Cascading Style Sheets, level 2 (CSS2), the current version of CSS, built on the previous version maintaining compatibility between currently conforming document browsers and their next generation.

NOTE   *Cascading Style Sheets level 3 has been under development since 1999, but as of October 2001 is not complete. You can follow the developments of CSS3 from the World Wide Web Consortium (W3C) Web site located at:* http://www.w3.org/Style/CSS/current-work.

The CSS1 and CSS2 specifications were based on design principles coming from the software development and graphic design and layout worlds. These principles include the following:

- **Independence.** Style sheets are not proprietary to a single vendor, platform, or device, enabling documents to work in all venues.

- **Forward and backward compatibility.** All Web browsers must be able to display the content of the document. CSS2 Web browsers are capable of displaying CSS1-formatted documents, just as CSS3-compatible browsers will support both CSS1 and CSS2.

- **Ease of updatability.** Style sheets complement the structure of documents so authors can change a style sheet with little or no change in the markup file.

- **Simplicity.** Style sheets are simple text files, easily read and written by document authors with a simple text editor.

- **Work with scripting of the DOM.** CSS properties can be accessed by JavaScript or VBScript programs through the Document Object Model (DOM). This allows for the dynamic update of the formatting of information. CSS3 will follow the dictates of the DOM2 recommendation, expanding upon support for events and other object references.

- **Accessibility.** Cascading Style Sheets provide a variety of features that make the Web more accessible for individuals with disabilities. Document visitors can create their own style sheet, overriding the author's style sheets, giving the reader the ability to ensure that the documents they read are legible for them. Users of Braille, embossed, and TTY media devices can have information tailored specifically to their equipment. Individuals using speech synthesizers or other aural devices can control the voice and audio output used. CSS3 plans include the improvement of accessibility features.

CSS Syntax

Cascading Style Sheets break individual style-sheet rules into two parts: a selector and a declaration, as shown in Figure C-1. The selector identifies the XML element, such as order or itemname, to which the rule is applied.

Selector   Declaration

Figure C-1   The selector and two-part declaration of every CSS rule.

The declaration has two parts: the property name and the value. The property name, found to the left of the colon, identifies the aspect of the selector being set (for example, the font or background-color of an itemname element). The value of the property, to the right of the colon, identifies the specific value used when adjusting the display of the element (for example, if the property is background-color, a value of black would force the itemname element to display on a black background).

CSS Properties

The following table lists the CSS2 properties:

ATTRIBUTE	VALUES (BOLD IS DEFAULT)
azimuth	angle | [left-side | far-left | left | center-left | **center** | center-right | right | far-right | right-side] | behind | leftwards | rightwards | inherit
background	[background-color || background-image || background-repeat || background-attachment || background-position] | **inherit**
background-attachment	**scroll** | fixed | inherit
background-color	color | **transparent** | inherit
background-image	uri | **none**| inherit
background-position	[**percentage** | length] | [top | center | bottom] || [left | center | right] | inherit
background-repeat	**repeat** | repeat-x | repeat-y | no-repeat | inherit

28

ATTRIBUTE	VALUES (BOLD IS DEFAULT)
border	[border-width || border-style || color] | **inherit**
border-bottom	[border-bottom-width || border-style || color] | **inherit**
border-bottom-color	**color** | inherit
border-bottom-style	border-style | **inherit**
border-bottom-width	border-width | **inherit**
border-collapse	collapse | **separate** | inherit
border-color	**color** | transparent | inherit
border-left	[border-left-width || border-style || color] | **inherit**
border-left-color	**color** | inherit
border-left-style	border-style | **inherit**
border-left-width	border-width | **inherit**
border-right	[border-right-width || border-style || color] | **inherit**
border-right-color	**color** | inherit
border-right-style	border-style | **inherit**
border-right-width	border-width | **inherit**
border-style	[**none** | hidden | dotted | dashed | solid | double | grooved | ridge | inset | outset] {1,4}| inherit
border-top	[border-top-width || border-style || color] | **inherit**
border-top-color	**color** | inherit
border-top-style	border-style | **inherit**
border-top-width	border-width | **inherit**
border-width	[**medium** | thin | thick | length] {1,4}
bottom	length | percentage | **auto** | inherit

ATTRIBUTE	VALUES (BOLD IS DEFAULT)
box-sizing	**content-box** | border-box | inherit
caption-side	**top** | bottom | left | right | inherit
cell-spacing	**none** | length | inherit
clear	**none** | left | right | both | inherit
clip	shape | **auto** | inherit
color	color | **inherit** | *system-color*
column-span	**integer** | inherit
content	[string | uri | counter | attr(x) | open-quote | close-quote | no-open-quote | no-close-quote]+ | normal | <uri> | check | diamond | menu-check | menu-diamond | radio | radio-on | radio-off | radio-ind | enabled-radio-on | enabled-radio-off | enabled-radio-ind | disabled-radio-on | disabled-radio-off | disabled-radio-ind | active-radio-off | active-radio-on | active-radio-ind | hover-radio-off | hover-radio-on | hover-radio-ind | checkbox | checkbox-on | checkbox-off | checkbox-ind | enabled-checkbox-on | enabled-checkbox-off | enabled-checkbox-ind | disabled-checkbox-on | disabled-checkbox-off | disabled-checkbox-ind | active-checkbox-on | active-checkbox-off | active-checkbox-ind | hover-checkbox-on | hover-checkbox-off | hover-checkbox-ind | **inherit**
counter-increment	[identifier integer] | **none** | inherit
counter-reset	[identifier integer] | **none** | inherit
cue	cue-before | cue-after | **inherit**
cue-after	uri | **none** | inherit
cue-before	uri | **none** | inherit

ATTRIBUTE	VALUES (BOLD IS DEFAULT)
cursor	[[**auto** | copy | alias | context-menu | cell | grab | grabbing | spinning | count-up | count-down | count-up-down | crosshair | default | pointer | move | e-resize | ne-resize | nw-resize | n-resize | se-resize | sw-resize | s-resize | e-resize | w-resize | text | wait | help] || uri] | inherit
direction	**ltr** | rtl | inherit
display	**inline** | block | inline-block | list-item | none | run-in | compact | marker | table | inline-table | table-row-group | table-column-group | table-header-group | table-footer-group | table-row | table-cell | table-caption | inherit
elevation	angle | below | **level** | above | levelbelow | higher | lower | inherit
empty-cells	**show** | hide | inherit
float	left | right | **none** | inherit
font	[[font-style || font-variant || font-weight] font-size [/line-height] font-family] | caption | icon | menu | messagebox | smallcaption | statusbar | window | document | workspace | desktop | info | dialog | button | pull-down-menu | list | field | **inherit**
font-family	family-name || generic-family list
font-size	absolute-size | relative-size | length | percentage | **inherit**
font-size-adjust	number | **none** | inherit
font-stretch	**normal** |wider | narrower | ultra-condensed | extra-condensed | condensed | semi-condensed | semi-expanded | expanded | extra-expanded | ultra-expanded]
font-style	**normal** | italic | oblique | inherit
font-variant	**normal** | small-caps | inherit

ATTRIBUTE	VALUES (BOLD IS DEFAULT)
font-weight	**normal** | bold | bolder | lighter | 100 | 200 | 300 | 400 | 500 | 600 | 700 | 800 | 900 | inherit
'group-reset'	<identifier>+ | **none** | inherit
height	length | percentage | **auto** | inherit
'key-equivalent'	**none** | (<key-press-combination>)+ | <system-key-equivalent> | inherit
left	length | percentage | **auto** | inherit
letter-spacing	**normal** | length | percentage | inherit
line-height	**normal** | number | length | percentage | inherit
list-style	[list-style-type || list-style-position || list-style-image] | **inherit**
list-style-image	uri | **none** | inherit
list-style-position	Inside | **outside** | inherit
list-style-type	**disc** | circle | square | decimal | decimal-leading-zero | lower-roman | upper-roman | lower-alpha | upper-alpha | lower-greek | lower-latin | upper-latin | hebrew | armenian | georgian | cjk-ideographic | hiragana | katakana | hiragana-iroha | katakana-iroha | none | check | diamond | menu-check | radio | radio-on | radio-off | radio-ind | enabled-radio-on | enabled-radio-off | enabled-radio-ind | disabled-radio-on | disabled-radio-off | disabled-radio-ind | active-radio-off | active-radio-on | active-radio-ind | hover-radio-off | hover-radio-on | hover-radio-ind | checkbox | checkbox-on | checkbox-off | checkbox-ind | enabled-checkbox-on | enabled-checkbox-off | enabled-checkbox-ind | disabled-checkbox-on | disabled-checkbox-off | disabled-checkbox-ind | active-checkbox-on | active-checkbox-off | active-checkbox-ind | hover-checkbox-on | hover-checkbox-off | hover-checkbox-ind | inherit

ATTRIBUTE	VALUES (BOLD IS DEFAULT)
margin	margin-width {1,4} | **inherit**
margin-bottom	margin-width | **inherit**
margin-left	margin-width | **inherit**
margin-right	margin-width | **inherit**
margin-top	margin-width | **inherit**
marker-offset	length | **auto** | inherit
marks	[crop || cross] | **none** | inherit
max-height	length | percentage | none | **inherit**
max-width	length | percentage | none | **inherit**
min-height	length | percentage | **inherit**
min-width	length | percentage | **inherit**
orphans	length | **inherit**
outline	[outline-color || outline-style || outline-width] | **inherit**
outline-color	color | **invert** | inherit
outline-style	border-style | **inherit**
outline-width	border-width | **inherit**
overflow	**visible** | hidden | scroll | auto | inherit
padding	padding-width {1,4} | **inherit**
padding-bottom	padding-width | **inherit**
padding-left	padding-width | **inherit**
padding-right	padding-width | **inherit**
padding-top	padding-width | **inherit**
page	identifier | **auto**
page-break-after	**auto** | always | avoid | left | right | inherit
page-break-before	**auto** | always | avoid | left | right | inherit
page-break-inside	avoid | **auto** | inherit
pause	[[time | percentage]{1,2}] | **inherit**

ATTRIBUTE	VALUES (BOLD IS DEFAULT)
pause-after	[time | percentage]| **inherit**
pause-before	[time | percentage]| **inherit**
pitch	frequency | x-low | low | **medium** | high | x-high | inherit
pitch-range	number | **inherit**
play-during	uri | mix? repeat? | auto | none | **inherit**
position	static | relative | absolute | fixed | **inherit**
quotes	[string string]+ | **none** | inherit
'resizer'	**auto** | both | horizontal | vertical | none | inherit
richness	number | **inherit**
right	length | percentage | **auto** | inherit
size	length {1,2} | **auto** | portrait | landscape | inherit
speak	**normal** | none | spell-out | inherit
speak-header	**once** | always | inherit
speak-numeral	digits | **continuous** | inherit
speak-punctuation	code | **none** | inherit
speech-rate	number | x-slow | slow | **medium** | fast | x-fast | faster | slower | inherit
stress	number | **inherit**
'tab-index'	**auto** | <number> | inherit
table-layout	**auto** | fixed | inherit
text-align	**left** | right | center | justify | string | inherit
text-decoration	**none** | [underline || overline || line-through || blink] | inherit
text-indent	length | percentage | **inherit**
text-shadow	**none** | [color || length] | inherit

ATTRIBUTE	VALUES (BOLD IS DEFAULT)
text-transform	capitalize | uppercase | lowercase | **none** | inherit
'toggle-group'	<identifier> | **none** | inherit
top	length | percentage | **auto** | inherit
unicode-bidi	**normal** | embed | bidi-override | inherit
user-focus	**auto** | normal | select-all | select-before | select-after | select-same | select-menu | inherit
user-focus-key	**auto** | normal | select-all | select-before | select-after | select-same | select-menu | inherit
user-focus-pointer	**auto** | normal | select-all | select-before | select-after | select-same | select-menu | inherit
user-inpu'	**none** | enabled | disabled | inherit
user-modify	**read-only** | read-write | write-only | inherit
user-select	none | **text** | toggle | element | elements | all | inherit
vertical-align	**baseline** | sub | super | top | text-top | middle | bottom | text-bottom | percentage | length | inherit
visibility	**inherit** | visible | collapse | hidden
voice-family	[specific-voice || generic-voice list] | **inherit**
volume	number | percentage | silent | x-soft | soft | **medium** | loud | x-loud | inherit
white-space	**normal** | pre | nowrap | inherit
widows	integer | **inherit**
width	length | percentage | **auto** | inherit
word-spacing	**normal** | length | inherit
z-index	**auto** | integer | inherit

CSS Example

The following example shows an external style sheet used to format the XML document shown in Figure C-2.

XML Orders Document

```
<?xml version="1.0" encoding="UTF-8"?>

<?xml-stylesheet type="text/css" href="orders.css"?>

<orderlist>

  <order>

    <name>R. Cypher</name>

    <company> Chimera Corp. </company>

    <address> 19 Driveby Ln., Alder, OR 99999
    </address>

    <item>

      <itemname> Paperclips </itemname>

        <itemdesc> Multicolored plastic paper clips
        </itemdesc>

      <itemvalue> 7.99 </itemvalue>

    </item>

    <item>

      <itemname> Legal Pads </itemname>

      <itemdesc> 8"x14" yellow narrow lined tear top
      pads </itemdesc>

      <itemvalue> 13.50 </itemvalue>

    </item>

    <ordertotal> $21.49 </ordertotal>

  </order>

</orderlist>
```

CSS Style Sheet

```
/*

 * Style sheet for use with Supply Orders

 */
```

```
order {
    padding: 12px;
    line-height: 2em;
    display: block;   }
name {
    font-size: 2em;
    color: blue;
    clear: left;
    text-align: center;
    display: block; }
company, address {
    font-size: 1.5em;
    margin: .83em 0;  }
itemname {
    font-size: 1.25em;
    margin: 1em 0 ;
    display: block }
itemdesc { font-style: italic; }
itemvalue { font-family: monospace }
ordertotal {
    font-size: 2em;
    display: block;  }
```

When applied to the orders.xml document, it will appear as shown in Figure C-2.

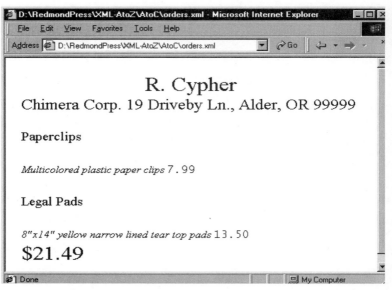

Figure C-2   Orders.xml with a simple style sheet applied.

SEE ALSO *<?xml-stylesheet?>, Style Sheets*

Case Sensitivity

XML is case sensitive. Although Cascading Style Sheet properties are not case sensitive, all element and attribute names in your XML document are. This means that an element named ORDER is a separate element than order. The DTD and/or XML Schema used to validate your XML document can validate your markup only if the element name(s), attribute name(s), punctuation, and letter-case in the document and the validation source match exactly. Any deviation will cause an error.

In addition to the names of items being matching for validation, attributes of the type IDREF and NMTOKEN require that the values specified match the exact case of the element or ID being referenced. Some scripting languages will also treat items with varying case as separate objects.

NOTE   *URLs may be case sensitive.*

SEE ALSO *Characters, Data Types*

CDATA see Data Types

CERN

The European Organization for Nuclear Research (CERN) is devoted to the development of standards for computer and other scientific endeavors. As a leading member of the World Wide Web Consortium and the "founders" of the World Wide Web, there are many standards, including the XML standard, which their involvement has improved. Many of the protocols we use today on the Web were originally developed and implemented at CERN before adoption in many other parts of Europe, including the ITU and the ISO in Geneva. By 1990, CERN had become the largest Internet site in Europe, dramatically improving the acceptance and spread of Internet techniques and standards around the world. All of this development led to the visionary idea of Tim Berners-Lee for the World Wide Web. In CERN's Internet facility, Berners-Lee developed the software portability techniques and the protocols to share information throughout the world.

Today, CERN promotes the development of Internet technology and training in developing countries, assists speakers at Internet gatherings, and works with the world authorities on Internet traffic and routing questions. You can read all about CERN on its Web site located at *http://www.cern.ch*.

SEE ALSO *World Wide Web Consortium*

CGI

The Common Gateway Interface (CGI) is the interface used between a server and the server-side gateway programs. This specification identifies how information is sent to, and returned from, to the gateway program. The main systems for performing this are as follows:

- **From server to gateway**—Data can be sent to the gateway as environment variables or as data read from standard input by the gateway program itself. The gateway reads all the data sent by the client and any extra environment variables that describe the current server status.

- **From gateway to client**—When returning information to the client program, generally a document or Web browser, the gateway writes the data to its standard output. When the client receives the data, it is processed to ensure that the headers are correct and that the information transaction occurred properly.

SEE ALSO *Perl, Scripting*

Character Encoding

Character encoding is a method of converting a sequence of bytes into a sequence of characters. When an XML application is encoded, it must use either UTF-8 or UTF-16 encoding. If the UTF-16 encoding scheme is used, then a Byte Order Mark must also be used at the beginning of the document. This encoding signature is used to differentiate between UTF-8 and UTF-16 encoded documents. You can read more about the UTF-8 and the UTF-16 character encoding schemes at *http://www.unicode.org*.

SEE ALSO *Entities, Unicode*

Character Set

A character set is a collection of characters, or glyphs, that represent all of the printable characters in the alphabet in one typeface and used in a document. Figure C-3 shows all the glyphs in the character set representing the Colonna MT font. Figure C-4 shows all the glyphs in the character set representing the Curlz font.

A B C D E F G H I J K L M N O P Q R S T U V W X Y Z
a b c d e f g h i j k l m n o p q r s t u v w x y z

Figure C-3   The set of characters representing the Colonna MT typeface.

A B C D E F G H I J K L M N O P Q R S T U V W X Y Z
a b c d e f g h i j k l m n o p q r s t u v w x y z

Figure C-4   The set of characters representing the Curlz typeface.

SEE ALSO *Unicode*

Comments

Comments within an XML document are the same as they are in person. They serve as a means of interjecting a sideline thought, or an instruction into a program at key points, so that no one looking at the document would ever find himself or herself lost.

Comments located within XML documents are identical to comments used within HTML documents. Comments use the <!— and the —> markers to identify the beginning and the ending of the comment, respectively. As with HTML, both the parser and the browser ignore everything contained within a comment as if it didn't exist. XML browsers will often specifically ignore comments, not even processing them.

The following XML example has a single comment shown in boldfaced text:

```
<?xml version="1.0" standalone="yes" encoding="UTF-8"?>

<order>

<!-- The name of the product being ordered. -->

    <itemname>Black Metal Stapler</itemname>

</order>
```

Using Comments to Block XML Code

The following comment provides auxiliary information to the contents of the XML file, but comments can also be used to remove segments of XML code that are not currently ready to be viewed or parsed, for example:

```
<?xml version="1.0" standalone="yes" encoding="UTF-8"?>

<!--

<order>

    <itemname>Black Metal Stapler</itemname>

</order>

-->
```

In this code, the only statement that will be processed is the XML declaration.

Rules for Using Comments

Comments within XML documents must follow these rules:

1. Comments can't appear before the XML declaration. For example, the following XML document would create a parsing error:

```
<!-- I have added a comment here. -->

    <?xml version="1.0" standalone="yes"
encoding="UTF-8"?>
```

```
<order>

    <itemname>Black Metal Stapler</itemname>

</order>
```

2. Comments may not split XML element tags. You cannot include the start tag of an element in a comment without including its ending element, or include an end tag without a start tag.

```
<?xml version="1.0" standalone="yes"
encoding="UTF-8"?>

<!--

<order>

-->

    <itemname>Black Metal Stapler</itemname>

</order>
```

3. You cannot include comments within XML element tags.

```
<?xml version="1.0" standalone="yes"
encoding="UTF-8"?>

    <order<!-- A comment is added here-->>

    <itemname>Black Metal Stapler</itemname>

</order>
```

4. Comments cannot include double hyphens within their text, unless those hyphens are part of either the opening or the closing tags. This prohibits the nesting of comments, as seen in the following example:

```
<?xml version="1.0" standalone="yes"
encoding="UTF=8"?>

<order>

<!-- This stapler is great <!-- I really liked it
also.--> -->

    <itemname>Black Metal Stapler</itemname>

</order>
```

Common Gateway Interface see CGI

Compound Documents

When you create XML applications, the actual document data can be stored in multiple files. When this is done, you are creating a compound document. In other words, you are combining an XML document, a style sheet to provide formatting, images to provide graphics, and, in many cases, a DTD (or Schema) that has been broken down into multiple pieces for ease of use throughout a corporation.

In order to create a compound document, two things need to happen:

1. The standalone attribute of the XML declaration must be set to "no," for instance, <?xml version="1" standalone="no"?>.

2. The individual files used to create the compound document must be accessible through the use of URLs on a local machine, or a network such as the Internet.

Compound Document Example

In the following XML document, you will find links to the orders.css style sheet document, the order.dtd document type definition, and an image for each of the items listed. The statements referencing external files are bold-faced in the example.

```
<?xml version="1.0" standalone="no" encoding="UTF-
8"?>

<?xml-stylesheet type="text/css" href="orders.css"?>

<!DOCTYPE orderlist SYSTEM "order.dtd">

<orderlist>

  <order>

    <name> R. Cypher </name>

    <company> Chimera Corp. </company>

    <address> 19 Driveby Ln., Alder, OR 99999
    </address>

    <item>

      <itemname> Paperclips </itemname>
```

```
       <itemdesc> Multicolored plastic paper clips
       </itemdesc>

       <itemimage url="images/paperclips.gif" />

       <itemvalue> 7.99 </itemvalue>

    </item>

    <item>

       <itemname> Legal Pads </itemname>

       <itemdesc> 8"x14" yellow narrow lined tear top
       pads </itemdesc>

       <itemimage url="images/legalpads.gif" />

       <itemvalue> 13.50 </itemvalue>

    </item>

    <ordertotal> $21.49 </ordertotal>

  </order>

</orderlist>
```

SEE ALSO *<?xml?>, Entities*

Conditional Statements

Document Type Definitions (DTDs) allow you to "comment out" unimplemented portions of your DTD. Two types of conditional statements are available with your DTDs: IGNORE statements, which prohibit the parsing of information in that section of the DTD; and INCLUDE statements, which force the inclusion, during parsing, of the material included in that portion of the DTD.

IGNORE
IGNORE statements force a specific section of the DTD to be ignored when the document is parsed. The format of an ignore statement is

```
<![IGNORE

   element and attribute declarations to be ignored

]]>
```

You can ignore any combination of elements, attributes, or entity declarations, but you must ignore a complete declaration. You can't ignore just part of the statement.

INCLUDE

INCLUDE statements force a specific section of the DTD to be included when the document is parsed. The format of an include statement is

```
<![INCLUDE

    element and attribute declarations to be included

]]>
```

When an INCLUDE statement is inside an IGNORE statement, the INCLUDE is also IGNORED. When an IGNORE statement is inside an INCLUDE statement, the statements inside the IGNORE block are still ignored.

SEE ALSO *Attributes, DTD, Elements*

Content Identifier see Entities

Content Model

Each element has a set of allowable content defined by the Document Type Definition (DTD) or an XML Schema. The content model of an element or attribute specifies within the document validation source which content is allowable for that element. The content model is specified in the element and attribute declarations in either the DTD or XML Schema that is used to validate the XML document.

As you may have noticed, some elements allow text content (ANY or mixed content), while others don't allow any (EMPTY). The content model specified within the DTDs <!ELEMENT> statement controls the content allowed for each element. An element's content model is specified with the syntax shown in the following table:

SYNTAX	EXPLANATION AND EXAMPLE
(...)	Delimits a group. <!ELEMENT order (item, name)
A | B	Either A or B occurs, but not both. <!ELEMENT order (item | name)>
A , B	Both A and B occur, in the listed order. <!ELEMENT order (name, company, address, items, ordertotal)>

C

XML From A to Z

SYNTAX	EXPLANATION AND EXAMPLE
A & B	Both A and B occur, in any order. `<!ELEMENT order (name & #PCDATA)>`
A?	A occurs zero or one time. `<!ELEMENT order (name?)>`
A*	A occurs zero or more times. `<!ELEMENT order (items*)>`
A+	A occurs one or more times. `<!ELEMENT order (items+)>`

When you use this basic syntax structure, you can create very complex sets of rules to control how your document information must appear.

```
<?xml version="1.0" standalone="yes"?>

<!DOCTYPE orderlist [

<!ELEMENT orderlist (order*)>

<!ELEMENT order (name, company, address, items+,
ordertotal)>

<!ELEMENT name (#PCDATA)>

<!ELEMENT company (#PCDATA)>

<!ELEMENT address(#PCDATA)>

<!ELEMENT items (lineitem+)>

<!ELEMENT lineitem (itemname & itemdesc & itemimage*
& itemcost)>

<!ELEMENT itemname (#PCDATA)>

<!ELEMENT itemdesc (#PCDATA)>

<!ELEMENT itemimage EMPTY>

<!ELEMENT itemcost (#PCDATA)>

<!ELEMENT total (#PCDATA)>

 ]>

<orderlist>

  <order>

    <name>R. Cypher</name>

    <company> Chimera Corp. </company>
```

```
<address> 19 Driveby Ln., Alder, OR 99999
</address>

<items>

  <lineitem>

    <itemname> Scissors </itemname>

    <itemdesc> Left-handed metal scissors
    </itemdesc>

    <itemimage address="/images/scissors.gif"/>

    <itemcost> 12.95 </itemcost>

  </lineitem>

  <lineitem>

    <itemname> Tape </itemname>

    <itemdesc> Scotch tape on plastic dispenser
    </itemdesc>

    <itemcost> 4.95 </itemcost>

  </lineitem>

</items>

<ordertotal> $21.49 </ordertotal>

</order>

<order>

  <name>K. Wizard</name>

  <company> Tualatin Paper </company>

  <address> 88 Mulberry Ln., Tualatin, WA, 99999
  </address>

  <items>

    <lineitem>

      <itemname> Paper </itemname>

      <itemdesc> Yellow legal pads </itemdesc>

      <itemcost> 7.95 </itemcost>

    </lineitem>

  </items>
```

```
<ordertotal> $65.89 </ordertotal>
  </order>
</orderlist>
```

SEE ALSO *Content Type, Data Types*

Content Type

The following table shows the valid content options for DTD element declarations:

CONTENT TYPE	DESCRIPTION AND EXAMPLE
EMPTY	Specifies that this element can contain no content, whether that content is text or child elements. `<!ELEMENT option EMPTY>`
ANY	Specifies that this element can contain any content, whether that content is text, child elements, or a combination of both. `<!ELEMENT order ANY>`
mixed content	Allows you to specify the exact content you wish the element to contain. You can specify only text data (#PCDATA) or a combination of text and specified child elements. `<!ELEMENT order (name | company | #PCDATA)>`
children	Specifies child element(s) that are found within the body of the identified element. This content can't contain any character data. `<!ELEMENT address (, street, suite, city, state, zip, phone)>`

EMPTY

The EMPTY designation specifies that no child elements or text content is allowed with this element. Empty elements must have a closing angle bracket at the end of each element declaration, as shown in the following statement:

```
<elementname />
```

EMPTY elements may contain attribute designations, and those attributes can have any kind of content. The following DTD shows the declaration of the empty element <itemimage> that has three attributes: address, height, and width.

```
<!ELEMENT itemimage EMPTY>

<!ATTLIST itemimage

    address #REQUIRED CDATA

    height CDATA "32px"

    width  CDATA "32px" >
```

The element would be displayed on an XML document in the following manner:

```
<itemimage address="/images/mygif.gif" height="15px"
width="15px" />
```

ANY

The ANY keyword allows an element to contain either child elements or text data or both with no restrictions. An element declared as containing ANY information could contain any of the elements in a document, without having those elements declared in the DTD or the Schema. An element declared using the ANY keyword would appear as follows in a DTD:

```
<!ELEMENT item ANY>
```

In the XML document, this element could appear in any of the following fashions:

```
<item> Scissors

    <itemdesc> Left-handed metal scissors </itemdesc>

</item>

<item> Paper </item>

<item>

    <itemdesc> Granite Rock </itemdesc>

    <itemimage address-"/images/myrockljpg"/>

</item>
```

Mixed Content

Mixed content declarations are somewhat like the use of the ANY keyword, but the child elements allowed are specifically declared, as shown in the following example DTD statement:

```
<!ELEMENT order (itemname | itemdesc | itemimage |
#PCDATA)>
```

In this case, the <order> element could contain only text content, that is, the itemname, itemdesc, or the itemimage elements. It could not contain a name element.

Children

Most elements allow child elements to be contained within them, but rather than let the ANY keyword allow any other elements, you can specify an exact content model for the specific child elements to be allowed. A sample DTD statement showing an element with a specific child element list, and content model is shown below:

```
<!ELEMENT lineitem (itemname & itemdesc & itemimage*
& itemcost)>
```

SEE ALSO *<!ELEMENT> Content Model, Elements*

Data Types

Data types set the type and style of information that can be contained within an attribute or an element. The following sections detail the data types applied to the contents of elements and attributes in DTDs.

CDATA

CDATA is character data used in an attribute. This is the most general type of attribute allowing any text string to be contained within the value portion of the attribute string. Strings can be composed of the standard letters and numbers (Aa–Zz, 0–9), and most punctuation characters. The only four characters excluded are greater than (>), less than (<), the ampersand (&), and the quotation mark ("). If needed, these characters can be represented by their entity references.

```
<!ELEMENT order CDATA>

<!ATTLIST order source CDATA>
```

In the XML document, an attribute of this type would appear as follows:

```
<order source=" just some text"> ... </order>
```

#PCDATA

#PCDATA is character data used in an element. This is one of the most common types of element content. PCDATA, like CDATA, can contain the numbers and letters Aa–Zz and 0–9, and all punctuation characters.

```
<!ELEMENT order (#PCDATA)>
```

XML documents use this element in the following manner:

```
<order> this is text data </order>
```

NOTE   *The greater than (>) and less than (<) characters should only be used to mark the beginning and end of child elements contained within the current element.*

ENTITY

The ENTITY data type links external unparsed entities to your document. An attribute of this type can only contain the name of an entity that is defined within your DTD.

```
<!ELEMENT order CDATA>

<!ATTLIST order source ENTITY>

<!ENTITY myentity SYSTEM "myfile.gif" NDATA GIF>
```

XML documents declare this element and attribute as follows:

```
<order source="&myentity;"> ... </order>
```

ENTITIES

The ENTITIES data type allows you to specify multiple entities in the value of an attribute, unlike the ENTITY data type, which allows only a single ENTITY to be specified.

```
<!ELEMENT order CDATA>

<!ATTLIST order source ENTITIES>

<!ENTITY myentity SYSTEM "myfile.gif" NDATA GIF>

<!ENTITY entity2 SYSTEM "myimage.jpg" NDATA JPG>
```

In an XML document, an attribute of type ENTITIES would be used in the following fashion:

```
<order source="&myentity; &entity2;"> ... </order>
```

ID

The ID data type creates an attribute for use as an identifiable name for referencing the element associated with the attribute.

```
<!ELEMENT order (#PCDATA)>

<!ATTLIST order idnum ID>
```

XML documents apply this attribute in the following fashion:

```
<order idnum="02-0988"> ... </order>
```

IDREF

The IDREF data type allows you to refer to previously identified ID type attribute values.

```
<!ELEMENT order (item)>

<!ATTLIST order idnum ID>

<!ELEMENT item (#PCDATA)>

<!ATTLIST item order_num IDREF>
```

XML documents implement these attribute types to link the item element to the order element logically.

```
<order idnum="99-00876">

<item order_num="99-00876"> Item information </item>

</order>
```

IDREFS

The IDREFS data type allows you to refer to multiple, previously defined ID type attribute values.

```
<!ELEMENT order (item*)>

<!ATTLIST order idnum ID>

<!ELEMENT item (#PCDATA)>

<!ATTLIST item order_num IDREF>

<!ATTLIST item item_num ID>

<!ELEMENT orderlist EMPTY>

<!ATTLIST orderlist item_nums IDREFS>
```

XML documents link all of the item elements to a single order by applying these attribute types:

```
<order idnum="99-00876">

<item order_num="99-00876" item_num="AZ876"> Item
information </item>

<item order_num="99-00876" item_num="AV456"> Next
Item information </item>

<orderlist item_nums="AZ876 AV456" />

</order>
```

NMTOKEN

This data type restricts the values of an attribute to well formed XML names which include text strings that start with either a letter (Aa–Zz) or the underscore (_).

```
<!ELEMENT item ANY>

<!ATTLIST item search NMTOKEN>
```

XML documents implement these types of attributes in the following fashion:

```
<item search="scissors"> ... </itemname>
```

This statement would create an error:

```
<item search="9scissors"> ... </itemname>
```

NMTOKENS

The NMTOKENS data type allows you to specify multiple NMTOKEN qualifying terms.

```
<!ELEMENT item ANY>

<!ATTLIST item searchterms NMTOKENS>
```

When used in an XML document, this attribute could appear as follows:

```
<item searchterms="scissors steel left handed"> ...
</item>
```

NOTATION

NOTATION type attributes are similar to ENTITY attributes but allow the attribute value to reference the name of a notation declared within your document.

```
<!ELEMENT itemimage EMPTY>

<!ATTLIST itemimage source CDATA>
```

```
<!ATTLIST itemimage software NOTATION ( GIF | JPG |
PNG)>

<!NOTATION GIF SYSTEM "psp.exe">

<!NOTATION JPG SYSTEM "psp.exe">

<!NOTATION PNG SYSTEM "fireworks.exe">
```

When used in an XML document, an attribute with a notation reference could appear as follows:

```
<itemimage software="PNG" source="/images/
myitem.png">
```

Enumerated Lists

The Enumerated list data type allows you to provide a list of possible text values for an attribute.

```
<!ELEMENT itemimage EMPTY>

<!ATTLIST itemimage imagetype ( image/gif | image/
jpeg | image/png )>
```

In an XML document, any of the first three statements would be valid, but the fourth would create an error.

```
<itemimage imagetype="image/gif" />

<itemimage imagetype="image/jpeg" />

<itemimage imagetype="image/png" />

<itemimage imagetype="image/bmp" />
```

NOTE   *Schemas use a wider variety of data types than DTDs. There are 45 predefined simple data types used with Schemas. All of these types are discussed under Schema Data Types.*

SEE ALSO   *DTD, Entities, Schemas, Schema Data Types, Validating Documents*

Database

Databases use a combination of tables, records, and fields to store information. Databases are commonly made of multiple tables that hold information related to each other. Take the following data chart, shown in Figure D-1, for example. In it you can see the contents of the Orders table, which tracks the client ID number, order ID number, shipping method, and payment type. The Items table holds the item number, the item description, price, and shipping weight. The LineItems table holds a list of item numbers that were ordered and item quantities. The Client table shows the client name, address, company, title, phone number, e-mail address, and payment information. The Shipping table tracks shipping organizations, shipping schedules, and shipping rates.

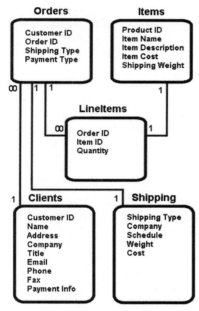

Figure D-1 Database structures.

SEE ALSO *Boolean Logic, SQL*

Databinding

The process used to bind, or connect, data information from a data source, such as a database, to an XML or other style of document. A variety of tools make this process easy, including the XML language itself used with either Java applets, server-side languages such as ASP or Cold Fusion, and XSL transformations.

SEE ALSO *Boolean Logic, Database, Document, SQL, XML, XSLT*

Dates

Dates in XML typically use one of the two following formats:
- year–month–day   2004–05–27
- month/day/year   05/27/2004

Dates are used in XML for a variety of situations, including tracking records, record information, tracking document creation and modification, and as part of record contents just to name a few.

Declarations

Declaration statements, are also called processing instructions. These are instructions to the document application itself. You can use them to control software settings. All declaration statements open and close with a <? and ?> marker. The following declarations are available with XML:

```
<?xml version="1.0" standalone="yes" encoding="UTF-8"?>
```

The XML Declaration statement is the first line of any XML document. It informs the document browser that the information contained within this document is XML text code.

```
<?xml-stylesheet type="text/css" href="mystyles.css"?>
```

This declaration, or processing instruction, associates a style sheet with the current document.

SEE ALSO *<?xml?>, <?xml-stylesheet?>, Processing Instructions*

Delimiters

Delimiters are markers in a document used to break apart information. For instance, a record delimiter in a database is the character, or character sequence, that shows the end of one record and the start of the second. In an XML document, the content delimiter is typically the opening and closing element of the content's containing element. Delimiters can be anything that separates one piece of information from another.

SEE ALSO *<!Element>, Boolean Logic, Database*

Digital Signatures

XML Digital Signatures provide a method of identifying the author, or origin, of a specific XML document. As of the fall of 2001, XML Digital Signatures is still in a working draft format. Check the World Web Consortium (W3C) Web site at *http://www.w3.org/TF/xmldsig-core/* to learn more about the constant development of digital signatures.

In the meantime, here is a quick example of the structure of an XML digital signature from the W3C Web site.

```
<Signature Id="MyFirstSignature" xmlns="http://
www.w3.org/2000/09/xmldsig#">

  <SignedInfo>

    <CanonicalizationMethod Algorithm="http://
    www.w3.org/TR/2001/REC-xml-c14n-20010315"/>

    <SignatureMethod Algorithm="http://www.w3.org/
    2000/09/xmldsig#dsa-sha1"/>

    <Reference URI="http://www.w3.org/TR/2000/REC-
    xhtml1-20000126/">

      <Transforms>

        <Transform Algorithm="http://www.w3.org/TR/
        2001/REC-xml-c14n-20010315"/>

      </Transforms>

      <DigestMethod Algorithm="http://www.w3.org/2000/
      09/xmldsig#sha1"/>

      <DigestValue>j6lwx3rvEPO0vKtMup4NbeVu8nk=</
      DigestValue>

    </Reference>

  </SignedInfo>

    <SignatureValue>MC0CFFrVLtRlk=...</SignatureValue>

    <KeyInfo>

    <KeyValue>

      <DSAKeyValue>

        <P>...</P><Q>...</Q><G>...</G><Y>...</Y>

      </DSAKeyValue>

    </KeyValue>

    </KeyInfo>

  </Signature>
```

Document

An XML document is an instance of an application of XML. The most basic XML document would have the following structure:

```
<?xml version="1.0"?>

<element>

    document content

</element>
```

An XML document doesn't have to be an actual file. It can be the results, stored in memory, of an SQL statement. It can be a collection of documents, or even a collection of search results. XML is strictly a way of formatting information so that it is easily read and interpreted by both people and computers. Most people prefer to think of an XML document as an actual file, because it is easier to envision using that basis for interpretation.

SEE ALSO *Applications, Dynamic Page Generation*

DOM

The Document Object Model (DOM) is the official model defining document structures for manipulation. All well-formed XML documents use the DOM. The DOM identifies the structure of your document as an inverted tree structure, shown for the following example document in Figure D-2.

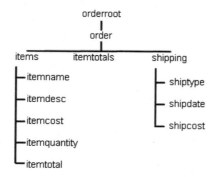

Figure D-2   Tree structure of an XML document.

```xml
<?xml version="1.0" standalone="yes" encoding="UTF-8"?>

<orderroot>

<order>

  <items>

    <itemname idnum="AZ9087"> Scissors </itemname>

    <itemdesc> Left handed, black handled metal
    scissors </itemdesc>

    <itemcost> 15.00 </itemcost>

    <itemquantity> 2 </itemquantity>

    <itemtotal> 30.00 </itemtotal>

  </items>

  <items>

    <itemname idnum="AZ0187"> Legal Pads </itemname>

    <itemdesc>

      Yellow lined, glue bound legal pads - Unit of
      10 </itemdesc>

    <itemcost> 14.00 </itemcost>

    <itemquantity> 4 </itemquantity>

    <itemtotal> 56.00 </itemtotal>

</items>

<items>

    <itemname idnum="DZ0457"> Chair Pad </itemname>

    <itemdesc>

      3' by 4' clear plastic hardwood floor protector
      </itemdesc>

    <itemcost> 13.00 </itemcost>

    <itemquantity> 1 </itemquantity>

    <itemtotal> 13.00 </itemtotal>

  </items>

  <itemtotals> 99.00</itemtotals>
```

```
<shipping>

  <shiptype> UPS 2nd Day </shiptype>

  <shipdate> 8/08/03 </shipdate>

  <shipcost> 4.99 </shipcost>

</shipping>

<ordertotal> 103.99 </ordertotal>

</order>

</orderroot>
```

Compatibility with the DOM ensures that style sheet languages, including Cascading Style Sheets (CSS) and XSL, work with your document, as well as popular scripting languages such as JavaScript and VBScript. Documents that do not follow the DOM will not parse properly, nor will they be able to have scripting events and styles applied properly.

You can follow the constant developments in the DOM by tracking the World Wide Web Consortium Web site located at *http://www.w3.org/DOM/*.

SEE ALSO *Scripting, Style Sheets*

DTD

Document Type Definitions (DTD) provide the key to validating your XML documents. DTDs serve as the recipe for the construction of an XML document. They control where, and how much, one item (element or attribute) can be added to the document. These documents, as shown below, contain the instructions that control how your document can be put together. A DTD contains a definition for every element, attribute, and entity used in the XML document.

```
<!DOCTYPE order [

  <!ELEMENT order (name, company, address, total)>

    <!ATTLIST order

        order_id ID>

  <!ELEMENT name (#PCDATA)>

    <!ATTLIST name

        type CDATA "billing"

        cust_id ID>
```

```
<!ELEMENT company (#PCDATA)>

<!ELEMENT address (#PCDATA)>

<!ELEMENT lineitem (itemname & itemdesc &
itemimage* & itemcost)>

  <!ATTLIST lineitem

      order_id IDREF

      cust_id IDREF >

<!ELEMENT itemname (#PCDATA)>

  <!ATTLIST itemname

      item_id ID >

<!ELEMENT itemdesc (#PCDATA)>

  <!ATTLIST itemname

      item_id ID >

<!ELEMENT itemimage EMPTY>

  <!ATTLIST itemname

      item_id IDREF

      source CDATA

      width CDATA

      height CDATA >

<!ELEMENT itemcost (#PCDATA)>

  <!ATTLIST itemname

      item_id IDREF >

<!ELEMENT ordertotal (#PCDATA)>

  <!ATTLIST ordertotal

      order_id IDREF >

]>
```

NOTE   *XML Schemas also define the recipe for creating an XML docu-
        ment. Schemas are newer than DTDs and are therefore only
        supported in the latest browsers: IE5.5 and NS6 and newer.*

You can use the same linked DTD for any number of documents that have the same structure. You can even link DTDs using entities to create compound documents that may combine an Order-based DTD with an Invoice-based DTD so that you can share the elements of each that are appropriate for the document you are creating.

SEE ALSO   *<!ATTLIST>, <!DOCTYPE>, <!ELEMENT>, Attributes, Compound Documents, Content Model, Data Types, Elements, Entities, Notations, Schemas, Validation, Well-Formed Documents*

Dynamic Page Generation

XML documents are generated in a variety of ways. The most obvious is with the hand creation of each document. Although this is typically how you would start the creation of an XML application, and how you would learn the language originally, you will find that as your application needs grow, the dynamic creation of a document using a server-side language, document scripting, and XSLT will become your best solution.

Server Side Languages

Server-side languages can dynamically create an XML document from the contents of a database, file, or other data source. Some of these server-based languages, or programs, include Cold Fusion, Active Server Pages (ASP), and Java Server Pages (JSP). These server applications allow you to enter information into a data file format, such as a database, and extract and format it as necessary to be displayed through your document, or Web, browser. Currently Cold Fusion, ASP, and JSP have been tested extensively with HTML, and developers are finding that they apply just as well to the creation of XHTML and XML documents.

Scripting

Scripting languages can alter the formatting and display of information in your documents. You can use JavaScript to test for the existence of a specific document viewer and format your document directly for the specific application viewing the document.

XSLT

XSLT transforms XML content into HTML content, or any other language you may wish to use, for viewing on a document browser. XSLT is a relatively new language that is still somewhat under development at the World Wide Web Consortium. You can read more about XSLT changes and development at the Web site *http://www.w3.org/Styles/*.

ECMA

The European Computer Manufacturing Association (ECMA) is just one of the standards organizations that works with the development of standards that are used on the Internet. In addition to the variety of information and communication systems standards that the ECMA develops, they have also created a standard for JavaScript/JScript as a way of alleviating the difficulty merging Netscape's JavaScript and Microsoft's JScript into single documents viewable by both browsers. Read more about the work of the ECMA at *http://www.ecma.ch/*.

SEE ALSO *ANSI, CERN, ISO, JavaScript, JScript, Scripting*

ECMAScript

The ECMA, with the help of companies such as Netscape and Macromedia, developed the ECMA 262 standard which creates an international standard for the development of the JavaScript language. Prior to the development of this standard, JavaScript "belonged" to Netscape and JScript "belonged" to Microsoft. Although JavaScript and JScript are very similar, and both languages use enough of the same functions and keywords that many scripts will function properly, there are enough variances that it is difficult, at best, to create any complex scripts that run well on both browsers.

SEE ALSO *ECMA, JavaScript, JScript, Scripting*

E-Commerce

Electronic commerce (e-commerce or e-business) is the manner in which purchases and sales are conducted through the Internet. In 2000, approximately $120 million worth of business was conducted over the Internet between consumers and businesses. Approximately $100 billion worth of electronic commerce took place between businesses.

XML is one of the primary formats for storing the information created during e-commerce interactions. Data stored in XML allows you to share the information among a variety of different database sources. You can use XSLT to create reports that sort out orders for specific items, without having to hire database developers and wait for complex queries and reports to be created. A sample XML-based invoice from an e-commerce transaction might look like the following example:

```
<?xml version="1.0" standalone="no" encoding="UTF-8"?>

<invoice>

  <customer>

    <name> R. Cypher </name>

    <address> 444 Titan Drive </address>

    <city> Toronto </city>

    <state> WY </state>

    <zip> 88888 </zip>

  </customer>

  <order>

    <items>

      <itemname idnum="AZ9087"> Scissors </itemname>

      <itemdesc> Left handed, black handled metal
       scissors </itemdesc>

      <itemcost> 15.00 </itemcost>

      <itemquantity> 2 </itemquantity>

      <itemtotal> 30.00 </itemtotal>

    </items>

    <items>

      <itemname idnum="AZ0187"> Legal Pads
       </itemname>

      <itemdesc> Yellow lined, legal pads - Unit/10
       </itemdesc>

      <itemcost> 14.00 </itemcost>

      <itemquantity> 4 </itemquantity>

      <itemtotal> 56.00 </itemtotal>

    </items>

    <items>

      <itemname idnum="DZ0457"> Chair Pad </itemname>

      <itemdesc> 3' by 4' clear hardwood floor
       protector </itemdesc>
```

```
    <itemcost> 13.00 </itemcost>
    <itemquantity> 1 </itemquantity>
    <itemtotal> 13.00 </itemtotal>
  </items>
  <itemtotals> 99.00</itemtotals>
  <shiptype> UPS 2nd Day </shiptype>
  <shipdate> 8/08/03 </shipdate>
  <shipcost> 4.99 </shipcost>
  <ordertotal> 103.99 </ordertotal>
 </order>
</invoice>
```

Electronic Data Interchange

This is a global term for the electronic systems used to exchange commerce information between businesses. These systems are based on database formats that were difficult to import and export into new systems. XML has improved on these systems by reducing the size of the information transferred between companies as well as making the import and export of the information faster and less complicated.

SEE ALSO *E-Commerce*

Elements

XML documents are primarily composed of elements. Elements comprise the markers that describe the contents of your document. For instance, the following itemname element lets you know exactly what the implication of the words "chair pad" have for this particular document.

```
<itemname> Chair Pad </itemname>
```

Declaring Elements

When declaring an element on an XML document, you get to decide the name of the element. For instance, you could be using an element to describe the name of an item for sale or an item on your to-do list. Either way, you get to make the decision about what you want to call your elements. For instance, all of the following element names are valid:

65

```
<itemname>

<TODOITEM>

<TakeHomeWork>

<Project_Step>
```

As you can see, you can not only give your elements whatever names you want but they can also be in any mix of letter case and underscore characters. However, they must be enclosed in angle brackets. The following section identifies the rules for naming elements.

Rules for Elements

The following are rules for elements:

- Names of elements can only contain the letters Aa–Zz, the numbers 0–9, and the underscore (_).
- Names must be included in angle brackets: <elementname>
- Closing tags must have a slash (/) preceding the name after the opening angle bracket: </elementname>.
- Element names are cases sensitive: for example, itemname, ItemName, and ITEMNAME are three different elements from the standpoint of the browser.
- All elements must have an opening and closing tag, unless it is an empty element: <itemname></itemname>.
- You can have as many elements in your document as you wish.

NOTE   *The names element and tag are often used interchangeably in documentation on XML. Technically, the element is the name (itemname) while the tag is the complete markup (<itemname>).*

Empty Elements

Empty elements are elements with no content. If you are familiar with HTML, the <img> element is empty. It has attributes such as src, width, and height used to describe it, but it has no content. The following is an example of an empty element:

```
<itemimage width="120" height="120" address="/images/
scissors.gif"/>
```

If the <itemimage> element were to have content, then it would appear as follows:

```
<itemimage> ... </itemimage>
```

Don't be confused by an element without content, and an element that doesn't allow content. For instance, you could have an empty <itemname> tag in your XML document, but it wouldn't be an EMPTY element. It would still have to be written rather than .

The DTD defines empty elements as EMPTY using the following notations:

```
<!ELEMENT elementname EMPTY>
```

Parent and Child Elements

When working with the tree structure of your common XML document, you will find that just like you, elements have parents and children. Take the following as an example:

```
<order>
<item>
</item>
</order>
```

In this example, the order element is the parent of the item element. The item element is the child of the order element. When specifying your elements in your document, you need to break down the information so that you have a variety of parent and child elements. You don't want a document where everything is on the same level. Take for instance the following example:

```
<order> </order>
<item> </item>
<itemname> </itemname>
<item> </item>
<itemname> </itemname>
```

In this example you don't know which items go with the order, and which item names go with which items. In order to group your information so that it makes logical sense to both the people reading the document and the computers processing the information, you must create a hierarchy, as shown in the following example:

```
<order>
<item>
   <itemname></itemname>
```

```
  </item>

  <item>

    <itemname></itemname>

  </item>

  </order>
```

Root Elements

Every document has a root element. The root element is the element that appears first, directly following the XML declaration, and last in the document. In the following example, the order element is the root element:

```
<?xml version="1.0"?>

<order>

  other elements and content

</order>
```

Element Content Model see Content Model

Encryption

Most information transported from a business to a business, or from a customer to a business, over the Internet is encrypted. In other words, it is encoded in such a way that no one watching information being passed back and forth over the Internet can read the information being shared. One of the most common situations for using encryption is the transfer of bank account and credit card numbers.

Encrypted information transferred over the Internet uses the Secure Sockets Layer (SSL) or Pretty Good Privacy (PGP) in most instances.

SSL

The Secure Sockets Layer (SSL), created by Netscape Communications Corporation, uses a series of digital certificates to identify and validate the identity of individuals and associations over the Internet. SSL is built into all major browsers, including Netscape Navigator, Internet Explorer, and Opera, and can be enabled for your XML documents, and document server, by the installation of a server SSL certificate. VeriSign (*http:// www.verisgn.com*) provides and sells SSL certificates for a variety of activities under two company names: VeriSign and Thwate (*http://www.thwate.com*). VeriSign manages the databases that provide verification of server identities when a server's SSL certificate interacts with a document browser.

PGP

Pretty Good Privacy (PGP) uses a public key and private key digital certificate system that allows you to send encrypted e-mail, including attachments, via the Internet to other individuals with a copy of your public key. Unlike SSL, which uses universally accessible databases controlled by the VeriSign issuing organizations, which verify the validity of the organization's identity, you must personally share your public key with individuals with whom you choose to share encrypted data. One popular use of PGP includes the submittal of encrypted form data from Web servers to electronic mailboxes. You can read more about PGP at *http://www.pgp.com*.

SEE ALSO *E-Commerce*

End-Tag

The end-tag of an XML element is the closing tag. Unless the element is empty, a closing tag will always have the following format:

```
</elementname>
```

SEE ALSO *<!ELEMENT>, Elements, Start-Tag*

Entities

Within XML, entities provide shorthand notation for including text or characters that would otherwise be difficult to implement in the application. Entities are often used to represent characters that can't be typed on a keyboard, or are specifically applied to other areas of XML document notation, such as the greater-than (>) and less-than (<) signs.

An additional use of entities is to represent boilerplate text. For instance, you can use an entity reference to identify a complete document's worth of information so that you don't have to manually write it on every XML document you build. For example, you can create a boilerplate entity of your copyright text, or even all of the contact information for your company.

Entities come in two main flavors: general and parameter. Either of these types of entities can be parsed or unparsed and be internal or external. Each of these combinations is discussed below.

External Entities

When including information from external sources, or sources outside of the current XML document, use external entities. External entities are typically associated with an URL that represents that external source. An example of an external entity is the src attribute of the HTML <img> tag. This tag/attribute combination is used to locate a file anywhere on a network, local computer, or the Internet that should be used in place of the current img element.

Internal Entities

Internal entities are completely contained within a single XML document. A document itself is an entity. Whether you create a document that is just the XML code or a document that is composed of the XML code in addition to a DTD, your document itself creates a single internal entity.

Internal entities can also be declared in a DTD that is included within the current XML document. For instance, if you declare an <!ENTITY> in your local DTD, the references to that entity in the XML code would create additional internal entities.

General Entities

General entities reference either internal or external entities, but no matter which, they add content to your XML document. General entity codes are replaced during parsing. The parser will substitute the information (text or file) represented by the entity name in place of the entity reference itself. General entity statements in your XML document will all appear with an ampersand (&) and then the entity name closed by a semicolon (;).

```
&entityname;
```

Internal General Entity Example

The following example of an internal general entity allows you to add your company's contact information to all your documents, without manually typing it into the document code.

```
<?xml version="1.0"?>

<invoice>

   &contactinfo;

</invoice>
```

DTD defines the &copyright; entity as follows:

```
<!ENTITY contactinfo "Wilbur and Deanna's Sales and
Shipping, 199 Tulsa Court, Tualatin, WY 88888">
```

When declared in a DTD, the general format of an internal general entity definition is

```
<!ENTITY entity_name "entity_value">
```

where entity_name is the name of the entity to be created and the entity_value is the text that will replace the entity name in the document during parsing.

NOTE   *You can use entities within entities, for example: <!ENTITY contactinfo "Wilbur & Deanna's Sales and Shipping, 199 Tulsa Court, Tualatin, WY 88888">. This example replaces the & in the entity declaration with an ampersand (&) symbol, and then replaces the &contactinfo; statement in the XML document with "Wilbur & Deanna's Sales and Shipping, 199 Tulsa Court, Tualatin, WY 88888."*

External General Entity Example

The following example of an external general entity would allow you to add your company's contact information to the bottom of all your documents, without adding it each time. This is the same as the previous example, but this time, the contact information is stored in an external file.

```
<?xml version="1.0"?>

<invoice>

   &contactinfo;

</invoice>
```

DTD defines the &contactinfo; entity as follows:

```
<!ENTITY contactinfo SYSTEM "contact.xml">
```

When declared in a DTD, the general format of an external general entity definition is

```
<!ENTITY entity_name SYSTEM "entity_URL">
```

where entity_name is the name of the entity to be created and the entity_URL is the address of the file that replaces the entity name in the document when parsed.

In this example, the contact.xml document would look like the following:

```
<contactinfo>

   Wilbur &amp; Deanna's Sales and Shipping,

   199 Tulsa Court, Tualatin, WY 88888</contactinfo>
```

NOTE   *The use of the & entity in the linked contact.xml document requires that the & entity is declared in the main document's DTD.*

Parameter Entities

Parameter entities also insert information into your XML document, but instead of being used in the XML document itself, they are used in the external DTD's associated with your XML document. Parameter entities combine multiple DTDs into a single application during parsing. This allows developers to modularize their DTD information so that you can have one DTD defining contact information, another defining order specific information, and yet another defining item information.

NOTE   *Parameter entities can only appear in external DTDs. They can't be used in internal DTDs or your XML document.*

Parameter entities are referenced in the DTD using the percent sign (%) as shown below:

```
%entity_name;
```

Internal Parameter Entity Example

Internal parameter entities are used like internal general entities. They create shorthand notations for lists of elements and attributes that are used multiple places in a DTD. The format of a parameter entity definition is as follows:

```
<!ENTITY % entity_name entity_definition>
```

Instead of defining the same set of child elements for two separate elements, as is done in the following example, parameter entities let you define it once.

```
<!ELEMENT ORDER (item+, shipping, total)>
<!ELEMENT INVOICE (item+, shipping, total)>
```

Using a parameter entity changes these declarations to

```
<!ENTITY % itemlist "item+, shipping, total">
<!ELEMENT order (%elist;)>
<!ELEMENT invoice (%elist;)>
```

NOTE   *Parameter entity statements must be defined before they can be used with an element or attribute.*

External Parameter Entity Example

External parameter entities insert a complete DTD into the current DTD. The format of an external parameter entity definition is as follows:

```
<!ENTITY % entity_name SYSTEM "entity_URL">
```

The combining of three DTDs would use the following external parameter entity statements:

```
<!ENTITY % customer SYSTEM "customer.dtd">
```

```
<!ENTITY % items SYSTEM "items.dtd">
```

In this example, customer.dtd contains the element and attribute declarations used for describing customers, and items.dtd contains the declarations for item information. These would be merged in the orders.dtd, which defines the order specific information.

Parsed Entities

Parsed entities are entities that can be parsed. All parsed entities are created from text files, such as XML documents or DTDs that can be processed by a parsing engine. Parameters are always parsed entities because they always contain DTD information. General entities are often unparsed, as they can contain nontext-based information.

Unparsed Entities

Entities that refer to information that can't be processed through a document parser, in the same fashion as a DTD or an XML document, are unparsed entities. Unparsed entity references commonly point to binary files, such as images or executable programs. Parameter entities are never unparsed entities. General entities can be unparsed entities.

Character Entities

General entities used to represent characters not available in the standard ASCII character set or that interfere with the processing of the XML document are often referred to as character entities. The standard character entities that have been defined for XML documents include the following:

ENTITY	CHARACTER
&amp;	Ampersand (&)
&apos;	Apostrophe (')
&brvbar;	Pipe, or broken vertical bar, sign (|)
&cent;	Cent sign (¢)
&copy;	Copyright symbol (©)
&current;	General Currency Sign (¤)
&deg;	Degree sign (°)

ENTITY	CHARACTER
&frac12;	Fraction one-half (½)
&frac14;	Fraction one-fourth (¼)
&frac34;	Fraction three-fourths (¾)
&gt;	Greater-than sign (>)
&iexcl;	Inverted exclamation point (¡)
&iquest;	Inverted question mark (¿)
&lt;	Less-than sign (<)
	Non-breaking space
&para;	Paragraph mark (¶)
&perc;	Percent (%)
&plusmin;	Plus-Minus sign (±)
&pound;	English Pound sign (£)
&quote;	Quotation Mark (")
&reg;	Registered trademark (®)
&sect;	Section sign (§)
&shy;	Soft Hyphen (-)
&uml;	Umlaut (¨)
&yen;	Yen sign (¥)

ENTITIES see Data Types

ENTITY see Data Types

Extensible Markup Language see XML

Extensible Style Sheet Language see XSL-FO

Extensible Style Sheet Transformation Language see XSLT

Formatting

XML documents have no formatting. In order to format your documents past the default tree structure shown in most Web browsers, as shown in Figure F-1), you have to provide a style sheet. Three main types of style sheets are applied to XML documents: CSS, DSSSL, and XSL. These style sheets are applied from external documents and either format the existing XML elements or transform the XML elements into another document format, such as HTML.

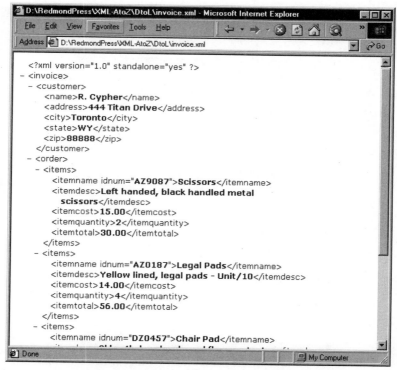

Figure F-1   Default document tree structure when viewed through a Web browser.

With a style sheet applied, you can format your document so that it takes on any appearance. You can format the document background to convert the XML data into block elements, as shown in Figure F-2, or you can make the information into a table format, as shown in Figure F-3.

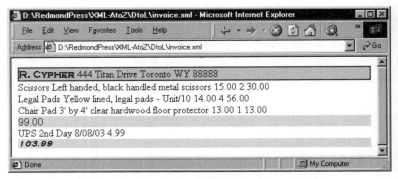

Figure F-2   Simple formatting of XML content using CSS.

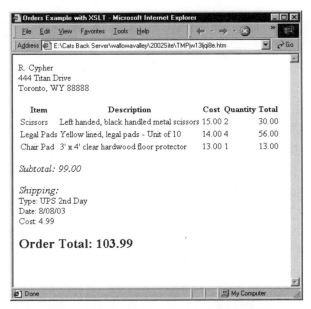

Figure F-3   More complex formatting of XML content into a table using XSLT.

All of these documents are based upon the following XML document:

```
<?xml version="1.0" standalone="yes"?>

<?xml-stylesheet href="invoice.xsl" type="text/xsl"?>


<invoice>
```

```
<customer>

  <name> R. Cypher </name>

  <address> 444 Titan Drive </address>

  <city> Toronto </city>

  <state> WY </state>

  <zip> 88888 </zip>

</customer>

<order>

  <items>

    <itemname idnum="AZ9087"> Scissors </itemname>

    <itemdesc> Left handed, black handled metal
    scissors </itemdesc>

    <itemcost> 15.00 </itemcost>

    <itemquantity> 2 </itemquantity>

    <itemtotal> 30.00 </itemtotal>

  </items>

  <items>

    <itemname idnum="AZ0187"> Legal Pads </
    itemname>

    <itemdesc> Yellow lined, legal pads - Unit/10
    </itemdesc>

    <itemcost> 14.00 </itemcost>

    <itemquantity> 4 </itemquantity>

    <itemtotal> 56.00 </itemtotal>

  </items>

  <items>

    <itemname idnum="DZ0457"> Chair Pad </itemname>

    <itemdesc> 3' by 4' clear hardwood floor
    protector </itemdesc>

    <itemcost> 13.00 </itemcost>

    <itemquantity> 1 </itemquantity>
```

```
    <itemtotal> 13.00 </itemtotal>

  </items>

  <itemtotals> 99.00</itemtotals>

  <shiptype> UPS 2nd Day </shiptype>

  <shipdate> 8/08/03 </shipdate>

  <shipcost> 4.99 </shipcost>

  <ordertotal> 103.99 </ordertotal>

 </order>

</invoice>
```

NOTE   *You can apply both XSLT and CSS, or XSLT and XSL-FO together to create a formatted XML document.*

SEE ALSO *Cascading Style Sheets, Style Sheets, XSL-FO, XSLT*

Heading

In XML there are no formatted headings, you have to use style sheets to create the appearance of headings. If your XML document is to be viewed in an HTML document browser, create the structure of headings using elements such as <h1> and <h2> from HTML. You can also use XSLT to transform your XML document into HTML. A third option is to apply a style sheet that will make the data have the physical appearance of a heading.

Hierarchies

XML documents are built in the style of an inverted tree. You have a single element that contains all of the other elements in the document. Every element is considered a node of the document. In a tree structure, each point in the tree is a node. For instance, in an invoice, the <invoice> tag would contain all of the other elements, including customer billing information, shipping information, lineitem information, tax amounts, and invoice totals. Take the following document for and example:

```
<order>

  <name>R. Cypher</name>

  <company> Chimera Corp. </company>

  <address> 19 Driveby Ln., Alder, OR 99999
  </address>

  <lineitems>

  <item>

    <itemname> Paperclips </itemname>

    <itemdesc> Multicolored plastic paper clips
    </itemdesc>

    <itemvalue> 7.99 </itemvalue>

    <itemquantity> 6 </itemquantity>

    <itemtotal> 47.94 </itemtotal>

  </item>

  <item>

    <itemname> Legal Pads </itemname>

    <itemdesc> 8"x14" yellow narrow lined tear top
    pads </itemdesc>

    <itemvalue> 13.50 </itemvalue>

    <itemquantity> 3 </itemquantity>

    <itemtotal> 40.50 </itemtotal>

  </item>

  <lineitems>

  <ordertotal> $88.44 </ordertotal>

  <shiptype> UPS 2nd Day </shiptype>

  <shipcost> 13.99 </shipcost>

  <totalcost> 102.43 </totalcost>

</order>
```

In the following table, you can see the relationship between each element in the document.

ELEMENT/NODE	PARENT	CHILD	ANCESTOR	DESCENDANT
order	–	company, address, lineitems, ordertotal, shiptype, shipcost, totalcost	–	company, address, lineitems, ordertotal, shiptype, shipcost, totalcost, item, itemname, itemdesc, itemvalue, itemqu-antity, itemtotal
company	order	–	order	–
name	order	–	order	–
address	order	–	order	–
lineitems	order	–	order	–
item	lineitem	itemname, itemdesc, itemvalue, itemquantity, itemtotal	lineitem order	itemname itemdesc itemvalue itemqu-antity itemtotal
itemdesc	item	–	item, lineitem, order	–
itemvalue	item	–	item, linietem, order	–
itemquantity	item	–	item, lineitem, order	–

ELEMENT/NODE	PARENT	CHILD	ANCESTOR	DESCENDANT
itemtotal	item	-	item, lineitem, order	-
ordertotal	order	-	order	-
shiptype	order	-	order	-
shipcost	order	-	order	-
totalcost	order	-	order	-

SEE ALSO *Ancestor, Node, Parent Element*

HTML

The Hypertext Markup Language (HTML) is the foundation of Web page design and implementation. Unlike XML, HTML can be displayed by all Web browsers. HTML provides its own formatting and content descriptions. Like XML, HTML is a derivative of the Standard Generalized Markup Language (SGML) and uses a series of elements, attributes, character references, and comments to identify and define portions of a document. A standard HTML document would appear as follows:

```
<html>

  <head>

    <title> document title </title>

  </head>

  <body>

    Elements and text content goes here.

  </body>

</html>
```

As you can see, a HTML document is broken into two sections, the head and the body. XML documents may be configured this way, but generally aren't.

SEE ALSO *Cascading Style Sheets, XML*

HTTP

The Hypertext Transfer Protocol (HTTP), used on TCP/IP-compliant client-server servers, is a set of rules that controls the exchange of HTML- and XML-formatted documents over the Internet. This protocol controls the interpretation of each element by document browsers. Typically, HTTP servers will use port 80 to transfer documents.

SEE ALSO *Servers*

Hypertext

Hypertext references the application of specific markup code, which allows for the linking of multiple documents. These links, also called hyperlinks, provide a document reader with the ability to quickly jump from one document to another at a click of the mouse. Links in XML documents are created using the XML Linking Language (XLink).

SEE ALSO *HTML, Markup Languages, XLink, XML, XPath, XPointer*

Hypertext Markup Language see HTML

Hypertext Transfer Protocol see HTTP

ID see Data Types

IDREF see Data Types

IDREFS see Data Types

Images

Images are pictures. They are the graphical elements that are associated with your XML document. Images in HTML and XML documents viewed through a Web browser can be of three types: GIF, PNG, and JPG. To add an image to an XML document, you would have to specify the image in a DTD as shown below:

```
<!ELEMENT itemimage EMPTY>

<!ATTLIST itemimage source CDATA>
```

```
<!ATTLIST itemimage software NOTATION (PNG)>

<!NOTATION PNG SYSTEM "fireworks.exe">
```

In an XML document, the statement loading your image would appear as follows:

```
<itemimage software="PNG" source="/images/
myitem.png">
```

SEE ALSO *Entities, Image Maps, Notations, XLink*

Image Maps

An image map is a combination of an image and a mapped-out collection of links. HTML uses the <img>, <map>, and <area> elements to create an image map. XML uses a collection of XLink notation and entities to create the same effect with any element. The entity is used to load the image, and the XLink notation creates the mapping of links over the image.

SEE ALSO *Entities, Hyperlinks, Images, Notations, XLink*

Inheritance

When working with Cascading Style Sheets (CSS), style inheritance is the manner in which styles are applied not only to the specified element but also to its descendants. Just as you could potentially inherit items from your parents, XML elements may inherit the styles that define their parent elements. For instance, if you have specified the <item> tag to have a gray background, then all its child elements would also have a gray background unless otherwise specified, as shown in Figure I-1.

Legal Pads - 10 Pack

6.99

Figure I-1   Inherited background colors.

```
item { background-color: gray }

<item>

    <itemname> Legal Pads - 10 Pack </itemname>

    <itemvalue> 6.99 </itemvalue>
```

```
</item>
```

Inheritance does not apply to all style sheet properties. These properties are as follows:

- border
- border-color
- border-style
- border-width
- margin
- margin-bottom
- margin-left
- margin-right
- margin-top
- padding
- padding-bottom
- padding-left
- padding-right
- padding-top

SEE ALSO *Cascading Style Sheets*

ISO

The International Organization for Standardization (ISO) is the main standards organization for the development of business protocols. Their membership includes 140 countries' national standards organizations. The ISO is not related to any government organization, allowing it to complete its mission of promoting the development of standardization with a view toward facilitating the exchange of goods and services internationally. You can get more information on the ISO from their Web site located at *http://www.iso.ch.*

SEE ALSO *ANSI, CERN, ECMA*

Java

Java was developed by programmers at Sun Microsystems as a way of controlling interactive televisions and VCRs. When the Internet exploded, engineers grabbed Java, called Oak at the time, and used it to develop a Web browser called WebRunner. This process progressed into the development of mini applications to use with WebRunner. In 1994 Oak was renamed Java. It had, by that time, grown into a full-fledged programming language with its own Virtual Machine. This meant that it could run anywhere, on any operating system, because it essentially took its own operating environment with it.

Java borrowed a lot of its syntax and structure from the C++ language. Unlike C++, Java is not compiled; it is interpreted. In other words, Java programs aren't converted to executable programs prior to its being run on your computer. There is one problem with interpreted programs, they tend to run somewhat less efficiently than compiled programs. Although Java is touted as being able to run on any operating system, with no changes to the code, this happens only if your entire application uses only Java. Any introduction of other languages will most likely limit the use of your application to one operating system. One reason that many developers use external languages in addition to Java is that Java lacks some core features, such as its own ability to print. In order to get around these obvious deficiencies, many developers create their own core Java programs and then create a series of modules that can access those missing features for each operating system.

NOTE   *Java is not related to JavaScript in any fashion, although there are some similarities in the syntax.*

JavaScript

JavaScript, originally called LiveScript, was developed by the Netscape Communications Corporation as a means of adding some scripting ability to Web pages. JavaScript, related to Microsoft's JScript, can be used to send information to Java applets, alter the contents of documents, load information proactively, and even identify the Web browser that is viewing the document.

JavaScript is an interpreted scripting language. It was designed to be simple enough for anyone with some interest and time to learn. JavaScript's syntax is very similar to C, so anyone already familiar with that language can start using JavaScript quite quickly.

In the mid 1990s Netscape began working with the ECMA to develop a standard scripting language for use in Web documents. The completed language is ECMA-262, or commonly called ECMAScript. ECMAScript is now the language referred to as JavaScript in the Netscape Navigator 6 browser.

SEE ALSO *ECMA, ECMAScript, Java, JScript*

JScript

JScript is Microsoft's version of JavaScript and ECMAScript. Microsoft's implementation of JScript 5.5 is a full implementation of the ECMAScript 3.0 specification, with some additional enhancements that work only with Internet Explorer.

JScript, in addition to providing basic scripting and automation services for Web pages, works with Microsoft ActiveX controls and Java applets.

SEE ALSO *ECMA, ECMAScript, Java, JavaScript*

Links see XLink

Markup Languages

Markup languages are used to mark specific sections of information contained within your documents. XML, HTML, XHTML, and SGML are all markup languages. SGML was the father/mother of these languages. The need for markup languages came from the requirement of many individuals to share information across university systems and business networks, when both sides of the transaction didn't have the same word processor. Markup languages are used to create headers, footers, paragraphs, code segments, captions, callouts, and other document sections without relying on the proprietary word-processing systems. With a word processor, the document has to undergo a conversion process for any other types of software to read the information, and even then the conversion of the document styles is not always exact. SGML and XML allow the document to be read by any type of software, with the document author being able to specify how each portion of the document's content will be interpreted by all software.

HTML/XHTML Markup Example

This example of a HTML/XHTML document simply identifies a head (head) and body (body) segment of your document, and then uses a paragraph (p) and two header elements (h1, h2) to define and format the content of your document.

```
<html>

<head>

  <title> Document Title </title>

</head>

<body>

  <h1> This is a level one heading </h1>

  <p> This is paragraph one. </p>

  <h2> This is a level two heading </h2>

  <p> This is paragraph two. </p>

</body>

</html>
```

XML Markup Example

This example of an XML document simply identifies the root element of the document (document) and then uses a paragraph (para) and two header elements (heading1, heading2) to define the content of your document. Unlike HTML/XHTML, XML does no formatting.

```
<?xml version="1.0"?>

<document>

  <heading1> This is a level one heading </heading1>

  <para> This is the first paragraph </para>

  <heading2> This is a level two heading </heading2>

  <para> This is the second paragraph </para>

</document>
```

SEE ALSO *HTML, Hypertext, XML*

Media Groups

Cascading Style Sheets (CSS) recognize 10 media types broken up into 4 media groups. These media types are applied to your XML document when it is associated with a CSS style sheet. The following table shows the organization of groups and types for your documents:

MEDIA TYPE	VISUAL/ AURAL/ TACTILE GROUP	INTERACTIVE /STATIC GROUP	CONTI-NUOUS/ PAGED GROUP	GRID/ BITMAP GROUP
All	all	all	all	all
Aural	Aural	Continuous	all	n/a
Braille	Tactile	Continuous	all	Grid
Embossed	Tactile	Paged	All	Grid
Handheld	Visual	all	all	all
Print	Visual	Paged	Static	Bitmap
Projection	Visual	Paged	Static	Bitmap
Screen	Visual	Continuous	All	Bitmap
TTY	Visual	Continuous	All	Grid
TV	Aural/ Visual	All	All	All

When formatting your XML documenting using CSS, you have the opportunity to adjust your formatting based upon the type of media that particular CSS properties are designed to work with. For instance, you can create a set of styles to control the formatting of a document for your computer screen, and yet another to control the playback of your document on a speech device.

The following sample style sheet modifies the same elements twice, once for screen display and again for aural devices:

```
@media screen {

    itemname { font: 4 red Arial;

               background: url('myimage.gif') }

    itemdesc { font: 3 black Arial; }

    itemcost { font: 4 black Comic Sans }
```

```
@media aural {

    itemname { voice-family: female;

            pause-after: 3 }

    itemdesc { volume: 2 }

    itemcost { azimuth: 5 }
```

SEE ALSO *CSS*

Media Types see Media Groups

META

The <meta> tag is used in many XML child languages to identify metadata, or information about the information, contained within your XML document. These elements can be used to identify simple things, such as the document author and copyright information, or even provide instructions to the document browser, as is shown in the following example.

```
<meta name="author" content="Heather Williamson"/>

<meta name="copyright" content="Copyright 2004. All
rights reserved."/>

<meta http-equiv="refresh" content="15;
url=nextdocument.xml"/>
```

SEE ALSO *MetaContent Framework, MetaInformation*

MetaContent Framework

MetaContent Framework (MCF) was begun by Apple's Advanced Technology Group and development continued under Netscape. This framework provided a three-dimensional browsing capability to Web documents, allowing visitors to view a tree of document links and progress immediately from one document to another without viewing each file in between. You can read about MCF's current state of proposal at *http://www.w3c.org/TR/NOTE-MCF-XML.html.*

SEE ALSO *Metalanguage*

Metadata see MetaInformation

MetaInformation

MetaInformation is a global term used to define the information that describes documents. A variety of types of information can be tracked, some of which are shown in the following table:

INFORMATION	META STATEMENT
character set identification	`<meta http-equiv ="charset" content="UTF-8"/>`
copyright information	`<meta http-equiv ="copyright" content=" Copyright 2002. All rights reserved "/>`
creation date	`<meta http-equiv="created" content=" 09/08/02"/>`
descriptive keywords	`<meta http-equiv="keywords" content="xml document, xslt"/>`
document author	`<meta http-equiv="author" content="H. Williamson"/>`
document server commands	`<meta http-equiv ="refresh" content="15; url=nextdocument.xml "/>`
expiration date	`<meta http-equiv ="expire" content="=" 03/08/03"/>`
modification date	`<meta http-equiv="modified" content="=" 012/08/02"/>`
rating systems identification	`<meta http-equiv ="rating" content="general"/>`
search engine identification	`<meta http-equiv ="description" content="my web site"/>`

SEE ALSO· *META, MetaContent Framework, Metalanguage*

Metalanguage

A metalanguage is a language used to describe other languages. XML markup is a metalanguage. Using XML tags, you create a document that literally describes its own content. In the case of a supply order, you would use the XML markup to identify the ordering party's name, separate from their mailing address, and still separate from the items they ordered.

```
<order>

  <customer>

    <name> R. Cypher </name>

    <address> Osborne, WY </address>

  </customer>

  <items>

    <lineitem>

      <itemname> Scissors </itemname>

      <itemcost> 5.99 </itemcost>

    </lineitem>

    <lineitem>

      <itemname> Paper </itemname>

      <itemcost> 1.99 </itemcost>

    </lineitem>

    <lineitem>

      <itemname> Legal Pads 10pk </itemname>

      <itemcost> 11.99 </itemcost>

    </lineitem>

  </items>

</order>
```

The XML tags <customer> and <items> break the document into two sections: one to describe the customer, and one to define the order being placed. The <name> and <address> tags complete the description of the customer, while the <lineitem> tag identifies an individual item that is being ordered, out of multiple items in the order. The XML tags <itemname> and <itemcost> provide the descriptive information, or markup text label, for the individual items that were ordered. <name> identifies the name of the person, in this case "R. Cypher," that the remaining information is discussing. This is meta information. A human would recognize "R. Cypher" as a person's name, but the computer can't. The computer requires that the document, or the application, tell it what this information is and how it is to be used or stored. XML uses the tag <name>. Once the computer knows what type of information it has, it can manipulate it to meet your needs.

SEE ALSO *Markup Languages, META*

MIME

Multipurpose Internet Mail Extensions (MIME) was originally designed to facilitate the transportation of audio, video, graphic, and other types of binary files over the Internet as attachments to e-mail messages. MIME is also used to identify file types that are used on the World Wide Web. MIME types must be configured on the document server, as well as in the document viewer's software, to work in their intended manner. The proper server configuration allows the document to be sent from the server without encountering errors, or corrupting the file, while the proper configuration on the user's machine allows the user to access the file immediately upon download.

SEE ALSO *Applications, Entities, MIME Types, Notations, Style Sheets*

MIME Types

Hundreds of MIME types are used on the Internet and with XML documents. The following table shows those that appear most often:

MIME TYPE	DESCRIPTION
application/msword	Microsoft Word-formatted document
application/pdf	Adobe PDF (Acrobat)-formatted document
application/pgp-encrypted	PGP-encrypted document
application/pgp-key	PGP encryption key
application/pgp-signature	PGP-encrypted signature
application/postscript	Adobe Postscript document
application/rtf	Rich Text Format document
application/sgml	SGML-formatted document
application/zip	Zipped file

MIME TYPE	DESCRIPTION
audio/basic	All basic audio files
image/gif	GIF image
image/jpeg	JPG image
image/png	PNG image
message/http	HTTP-formatted message
message/nntp	Newsgroup message
multipart/encrypted	Encrypted message with some unencrypted material
multipart/formdata	Results of a form submittal
multipart/mixed	Contains multiple types of information
text/css	Cascading Style Sheet document
text/html	HTML-formatted text file
text/plain	Plain ASCII text file
text/richtext	Text file using the RTF extension
text/sgml	SGML-formatted file
text/xsl	Extensible Style Sheet document
video/mpeg	MPEG-formatted video
video/quicktime	Apple QuickTime movie

SEE ALSO *MIME, Notations*

Mixed-Content Declaration see Elements

MSXML

Microsoft XML (MSXML) is the parsing program added to Microsoft's Internet Explorer browser to parse and validate XML documents. If you are using Internet Explorer to work with and test your XML documents, be sure to download the latest version of MSXML for your browser from *http://msdn.Microsoft.com/xml/default.asp.*

SEE ALSO *Parsers, XML Software*

93

Multi-Directional Links see XLink

Namespaces

The XML Namespaces recommendation, released in January 1999, specifies the rules for associating element and attribute names used in an XML document with a collection of element and attribute names identified, often in DTD form, by a specific Uniform Resource Identifier (URI). XML Namespaces creates a mechanism in which a single document uses the elements and attributes identified for other documents, without worrying about duplication of element and attribute names. This system adds a prefix to the names of elements and attributes so that each is properly associated with its originating document, which is in turn associated with that prefix.

NOTE   *Read the specification on the World Wide Web Consortium (W3C) Web site located at* http://www.w3.org/ TR/1999/REC-xml-names-19990114/.

Identifying Namespaces

XML Namespaces use the xmlns notation to identify namespaces associated with elements. This notation differentiates between the local names already included in your document's current DTD and those being referenced from other DTDs.

The xmlns notation is used in the following manner:

```
<elementname xmlns:prefix="namespaceurl">
```

For instance:

```
<math xmlns:mathml="http://www.w3.org/TR/REC-MathML">
```

This format uses a mapping system already acceptable in XML, where you use a prefix to identify the namespace being associated with the element or attribute. The namespace prefix used with the xmlns notation identifies the source of the DTD used to fully identify this universal attribute, in this case the MathML specification.

NOTE   *You can't use either xml (xmlns:xml) or xmlns (xmlns:xmlns) as your prefix notation to bind a namespace to a document. The xml prefix, by default, points to the* http://www.w3.org/XML/1998/ namespace *address for the XML document itself. The xmlns prefix is used to bind elements to namespaces.*

More specifically, the namespace declaration associates the specified element or attribute to the namespace prefix representing the namespace located at the specified URL. This allows the customers element in one document type to be used in another document with its own customers element without creating validation errors, while also allowing elements from multiple document definitions to be used in the same XML document.

The following example code should help clarify this situation:

```xml
<?xml version="1.0"?>

<orders xmlns:ord="http://myserver.com/dtds/orders/">

  <customers xmlns:cust="http://myserver.com/dtds/
  customers/">

    <cust:name> R. Cypher </cust:name>

    <cust:address> 444 Titan Drive </cust:address>

    <cust:city> Toronto </cust:city>

    <cust:state> WY </cust:state>

    <cust:zip> 88888 </cust:zip>

  </customers>

  <ord:items>

    <ord:itemname idnum="AZ9087"> Scissors
      </ord:itemname>

    <ord:itemdesc> Left handed, black handled metal
      scissors </ord:itemdesc>

    <ord:itemcost> 15.00 </ord:itemcost>

    <ord:itemquantity> 2 </ord:itemquantity>

    <ord:itemtotal> 30.00 </ord:itemtotal>

  </ord:items>

  <ord:items>

    <ord:itemname idnum="AZ0187"> Legal Pads
      </ord:itemname>

    <ord:itemdesc> Yellow lined, legal pads - Unit of
      10 </ord:itemdesc>

    <ord:itemcost> 14.00 </ord:itemcost>

    <ord:itemquantity> 4 </ord:itemquantity>

    <ord:itemtotal> 56.00 </ord:itemtotal>
```

```
      </ord:items>

      < ord:items>

          <ord:itemname idnum="DZ0457"> Chair Pad
            </ord:itemname>

          <ord:itemdesc> 3'x4' clear plastic floor
            protector </ord:itemdesc>

          <ord:itemcost> 13.00 </ord:itemcost>

          <ord:itemquantity> 1 </ord:itemquantity>

          <ord:itemtotal> 13.00 </ord:itemtotal>

      </ord:items>

      <ord:itemtotals> 99.00</ord:itemtotals>

      <ord:shipping>

          <ord:shiptype> UPS 2nd Day </ord:shiptype>

          <ord:shipdate> 8/08/03 </ord:shipdate>

          <ord:shipcost> 4.99 </ord:shipcost>

      </ord:shipping>

      <ord:ordertotal> 103.99 </ord:ordertotal>

  </order>
```

NOTE   *Although the previous example is well formed, it is not a valid document. When using multiple namespace declarations (or prefixes) within a validating processor on a single document, errors will occur. Most XML applications do not currently validate documents using namespaces. In order for namespaces to be used you must use qualified namespace declarations within a subset of the DTD, for instance, <!ELEMENT ord:ordertotal #PCDATA>.*

In the preceding example, the <order> and the <customer> elements use namespace declarations to identify the various XML elements used in the markup. These declaration statements imply that all order child elements, attributes, and contents will be bound to *http://myserver.com/dtds/orders/*. Just as all customer child elements, attributes, and contents are bound to *http://myserver.com/dtds/customers/*.

NOTE   *It is unnecessary to declare a namespace for each child element as long as the parent element has been declared. The namespace is automatically applied to the child element and all of the attributes of those elements, unless otherwise specified.*

Namespace Rules

Namespaces must be compatible with the following rules:

- Qualified names are a combination of the prefix and local element name, for example, <cust:name> or <ord:items>. In each of these cases, you can easily differentiate between various elements that appear in the specifications from both sources.

NOTE   *The prefix is a placeholder for the namespace name. When creating a document whose scope extends past the local document, use the full URL of the namespace in place of the prefix.*

- A qualified attribute applies the prefix directly to the attribute name, for instance, <order ord:ordid="99-8756">.

- Qualified element names must have the prefix applied to both the opening and closing tags: <ord:items> and </ord:items>.

- If you are qualifying an attribute within an element, you only need to apply the prefix to the name of the attribute: <items ord:itemnum="99-0087">.

Default Namespaces

A default namespace is applied to an element without a currently defined prefix. If the URL has been left blank in an xmlns: declaration, then that element and any of its children without an explicitly defined namespace will be considered to be in the default namespace.

NOTE   *Default namespaces do not apply to attributes. All attributes must be explicitly defined using a namespace prefix, unless they are part of an element with a qualified prefix.*

In the following example, all of the elements have inherited the default namespace defined by the xmlns statement, because no other prefix has been defined and the elements are direct children of the root element.

```
<?xml version="1.0"?>

<customers xmlns:cust="http://myserver.com/dtds/
customers/">

  <cust:name> R. Cypher </cust:name>

  <cust:address> 444 Titan Drive </cust:address>
```

97

```
<cust:city> Toronto </cust:city>

<cust:state> WY </cust:state>

<cust:zip> 88888 </cust:zip>

</customers>
```

This document would be treated the same as the previous example because only the root element has a declared namespace:

```
<?xml version="1.0"?>

<customers xmlns:cust="http://myserver.com/dtds/
customers/">

    <name> R. Cypher </name>

    <address> 444 Titan Drive </address>

    <city> Toronto </city>

    <state> WY </state>

    <zip> 88888 </zip>

</customers>
```

Adding Namespaces to DTDs

Incorporating a namespace declaration into a DTD can create as many problems as it solves. The xmlns: prefix declaration is treated as an attribute by the XML processor, forcing its definition within the document's DTD or Schema. One means of defining the namespace is to use the following statement:

```
<!ATTLIST ELEMENTNAME xmlns:prefix "namespace URL"
#IMPLIED>
```

If you apply this attribute to the root element of a document, then the namespace is available to all of the root element's children and attributes. Because a namespace declaration applies to the element in which it is identified, and all of that element's child elements, attributes, and contents, you may declare multiple namespaces for a single element declaration. This makes both declarations available and valid for each child element and attribute.

```
<!ATTLIST order xmlns:ord "/dtd/orders/" #IMPLIED

                xmlns:cust "/dtd/customers/" #IMPLIED

                xmlns:items "/dtd/items/" #IMPLIED>
```

In addition to using multiple namespaces in a single XML document, to merge document structure, multiple namespaces can merge multiple DTDs together into one format and validate your contents simultaneously. To do this, modularize your DTD and place the declarations for those modules into your document. Look at the following DTDs. The first is for an order, the second is for the order items, and the third is for a customer record.

The Order's DTD

```
<!ELEMENT order (lineitem & customer & ordertotal)>

    <!ATTLIST order

        order_id ID

        cust_id IDREF >

  <!ELEMENT ordertotal (#PCDATA)>

    <!ATTLIST ordertotal

        order_id IDREF >
```

The DTD for the Items

```
<!ELEMENT lineitem (itemname & itemdesc & itemimage*
& itemcost)>

    <!ATTLIST lineitem

        order_id IDREF

        cust_id IDREF >

  <!ELEMENT itemname (#PCDATA)>

    <!ATTLIST itemname

        item_id ID >

  <!ELEMENT itemdesc (#PCDATA)>

    <!ATTLIST itemname

        item_id ID >

  <!ELEMENT itemimage EMPTY>

    <!ATTLIST itemname

        item_id IDREF

        source CDATA

        width CDATA

        height CDATA >
```

```
<!ELEMENT itemcost (#PCDATA)>

  <!ATTLIST itemname

      item_id IDREF >
```

The Customer's DTD

```
<!ELEMENT customer (name, company, address)>

  <!ATTLIST customer

      cust_id ID>

<!ELEMENT name (#PCDATA)>

  <!ATTLIST name

      type CDATA "billing"

      cust_id ID>

<!ELEMENT company (#PCDATA)>

<!ELEMENT address (#PCDATA)>
```

Once each DTD has been developed, you need to incorporate all of them into your document by identifying them with namespaces and incorporating those into your base document declaration in the following fashion:

```
<o:order xmlns:ord="order.dtd"

      xmlns:items="item.dtd"

      xmlns:cust="customer.dtd"  >
```

Naming Conventions

The following are rules for naming either elements or attributes used in XML documents:

- Names can only start with letters Aa–Zz or the underscore (_).
- After the first letter, only the letters Aa–Zz, numbers 0–9, the underscore (_), hyphen (-), and period (.) may be used.
- Names cannot include white spaces.
- Names are case sensitive: for example, itemname, ItemName, and ITEMNAME are three different elements from the standpoint of the browser.

SEE ALSO *Attributes, Elements*

Nesting

XML documents use nested elements to create a logical structure for your information, which is referred to as a document hierarchy. Just as in genealogy, each element on an XML document is treated like a node on a tree, inverted in this case, where more elements and content can branch off. In the following example, the itemname, itemdesc, itemcost, itemquantity, and itemtotal elements are nested in the items element. The items element is in turn nested in the lineitems element.

```
<lineitems>

  <items>

    <itemname idnum="DZ0457"> Chair Pad </itemname>

    <itemdesc> 3'x4' clear plastic floor protector
      </itemdesc>

    <itemcost> 13.00 </itemcost>

    <itemquantity> 1 </itemquantity>

    <itemtotal> 13.00 </itemtotal>

  </items>

</lineitems>
```

In an XML document, this type of nesting can continue indefinitely. Although for readability, of people, you may want to consider keeping the nesting to fewer than 7 levels of information. The computer doesn't care if you have 100 layers of nesting.

SEE ALSO *Ancestor, Hierarchies, Node, Parent Elements, Tree Structures*

NMTOKEN see Data Types

NMTOKENS see Data Types

Node

A document node, as considered by the tree structure of an XML document, is an element. In a document tree, a node is a point at which other nodes can be created. In Figure N-1, the nodes are shown as varying levels in an inverted tree document.

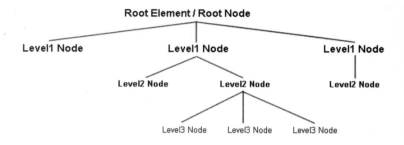

Figure N-1   Node tree structure.

SEE ALSO *Ancestor, Hierarchies, Nesting, Parent Elements, Tree Structure*

Normalization

Normalization is the process of breaking down the information in a database into the smallest unique parts, as a means of alleviating any difficulties associated with reentering information multiple times. XML documents can also be normalized by using elements and attributes to break down the contents of your document into as many logical forms, using elements, as is required to be able to access each portion of your document without filtering.

For instance, the following example is normalized because you can access any piece of information contained within the document without filtering strings:

```
<name>

  <fname> Richard </fname>

  <minit> F </minit>

  <lname> Cypher </lname>

</name>
```

This next example isn't normalized. In order to recover the client's last name for sorting or labeling purposes, you will have to run a script to separate it from the remainder of the information.

```
<name> Richard F. Cypher </name>
```

SEE ALSO *Database*

NOTATION see Data Types

Notations

The widespread source of information formats, ranging from Microsoft Word files to Real Player video- and audio-formatted files, makes it imperative that XML work with and incorporate information in its current binary form. Notations allow you to identify the type of file, any file, you are adding to your document.

There is no way for an XML document to identify a JPEG image separate from a GIF image using its entity, element, or attribute markup. The software reading your XML document therefore has to be told what kind of data is stored in your files.

In addition to identifying the format of your information, notations also inform the XML application of how to read and display the file's contents. Notations help prevent your XML browser from displaying a zip file on your screen while the information is still compressed. Notations separate the type of information contained within a file, from the file itself, allowing the XML software to work properly with the file's contents.

NOTE   *You can create XML documents without using notations. Some groups don't believe that these constructs should be a part of the XML specification. You must decide whether you wish to use these constructs in your documents. If you do use them, be aware that few XML applications currently support them.*

Notation Syntax

The declaration statement used to identify a notation is similar to that used to declare an external entity. You provide a name for the file type, use either the SYSTEM or PUBLIC identifier, and then provide an external identifier for the file type, as seen in the example syntax statement shown below:

```
<!NOTATION file_type (SYSTEM|PUBLIC "public id")
"external_identifier">
```

This basic notation can be used to identify a series of image types, including BMP, GIF, and JPEG, as shown in the following example:

```
<!NOTATION BMP SYSTEM "image/bitmap">

<!NOTATION GIF SYSTEM "image/gif">

<!NOTATION JPEG SYSTEM "image/jpg">
```

103

In these statements, the MIME-type of the image is the external identifier of the element. There are many other possibilities, including a standard URL or the use of a PUBLIC identifier and a URI. To use PUBLIC identifiers, be familiar with the public identifier system available from the Internet Engineering Task Force (IETF) (*http://www.ietf.org*). The following notation identifies a JPEG image using the PUBLIC identifier for the JPEG standard created by the IETF:

```
<!NOTATION JPEG PUBLIC "-//IETF//NONSGML Media Type
image/jpeg//EN""http://www.isi.edu/in-notes/iana/
assignments/media-types/images/jpeg">
```

So far everything from MIME types to URLs and ISBN numbers have been used to describe a notation. Other sources have used card catalog numbers as well as International Standards Organization (ISO) standard identifiers. There are no restrictions on the use of identifiers, but choose wisely. Take into account that URLs change often, so if you expect your document to last a decade, you may wish to identify it based upon a resource other than a Web URL.

Notation Example

In addition to identifying information that is not XML data, you can identify XML formattable information. One good example of this is dates. How can you tell the meaning of one date from another? Take for example 05-12-01. Is this date May 12, 2001? Is it meant to represent December 1, 2005? Or is it meant to be December 5, 2001?

Documents must be able to specify the format of dates so they will be properly interpreted. Using notations, you can specify any format for the dates you use, either as a standard date format, such as MM-DD-YY, or simply as a type of date, such as Gregorian based upon ISO standard 8601. The following example uses three formats of dates that allow you to properly interpret the formatting of the dates found within the document.

NOTE   *For more information on using Data Types in DTDs, check out the World Wide Web Consortium (W3C) Web site at* http://www.w3.org/TR/dt4dtd.

```
<?xml version="1.0"?>

<!DOCTYPE order [

  <!ELEMENT order (order_date, shipping_date)

  <!ELEMENT order_date (#PCDATA)>
```

```
    <!ATTLIST order_date system NOTATION (SHORT |
    LONG | GREGORIAN) #IMPLIED>

<!ELEMENT shipping_date (#PCDATA)>

    <!ATTLIST shipping_date system NOTATION (SHORT |
    LONG | GREGORIAN) #IMPLIED>

<!NOTATION GREGORIAN SYSTEM "http://myserver.com/
dateformat/gregorian/">

<!NOTATION SHORT SYSTEM "http://myserver.com/
dateformat/short/">

<!NOTATION LONG SYSTEM "http://myserver.com/
dateformat/long/">

]>

<order>

    <order_date system="SHORT"> 05/31/04 </order_date>

    <shipping_date system="LONG"> May 31, 2004
    </shipping_date>

</order>
```

NOTE   *Notations can't force document authors to display their informa-
        tion in the correct format, they can only remind authors of the
        format that they should use. XML Schemas are currently the only
        validation format that can restrict the contents of your elements.*

SEE ALSO *Attributes, Entities*

Parent Elements

XML document structure derives from the concept of a tree structure. In this
system, a parent is an element that directly precedes the current element in
the document tree. In the following example document, the items element
is an ancestor of the itemname element, just as order is the parent of the items
element.

```
<?xml version="1.0" standalone="yes" encoding="UTF-
8"?>

<order>

    <name> R. Cypher </name>

    <items>

        <itemname> Legal Pads - 10 Pack </itemname>
```

```
<itemvalue> 6.99 </itemvalue>

</items>

</order>
```

As you can see in Figure P-1, the similarity of the XML document tree to a standard genealogical tree makes the identification of parents quite simple.

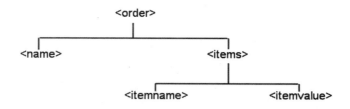

Figure P-1   XML document tree structure.

SEE ALSO *Ancestor, Hierarchies, Node, Tree Structure*

Parsers

The primary type of software you are concerned with when dealing with XML documents is the parser. Parsers process the information contained within the XML document, and if capable, verify the structure of the XML against either a DTD or a Schema document. There are two distinct types of parsers: nonvalidating and validating.

Nonvalidating Parsers

Nonvalidating parsers are the most common, and they are the simplest to write XML documents for. Nonvalidating parsers simply check for well-formedness within your XML document. These parsers ensure that you have dotted your "i's" and crossed your "t's." They do not ensure that your XML tags are proper, since they don't know which tags are allowed in your document and which aren't. Nonvalidating parsers ensure that for every opening XML tag you have a closing tag, or that your tag has been formatted as an empty tag.

A variety of nonvalidating parsers are available. For example, Internet Explorer version 5 has a built-in parser that checks for well-formedness, without validating the actual XML document code, although you can download a validating version of their parser if you wish (*http://msdn.Microsoft.com/*

xml/default.asp). Netscape Navigator 6 includes a parser, but it requires that you have a style sheet associated with the document before it can display your XML data. This joining of document browser and parser is a nice combination allowing you to completely check your XML documents in one package, rather than having to check the document for well-formedness using one piece of software and requiring a second set to view the output.

Using Internet Explorer to Parse Your XML

To use Internet Explorer to parse your XML document, follow these steps:

1. Open up Internet Explorer 5 by selecting Start→Programs→Internet Explorer in Windows, or selecting its icon from your Macintosh drive or desktop.

2. Open a sample XML document by selecting File→Open and then use the Browse button to select an XML document on your computer.

If the document you chose to view has no parsing errors, and no associated style sheet, it will appear similar to what is shown in Figure P-2.

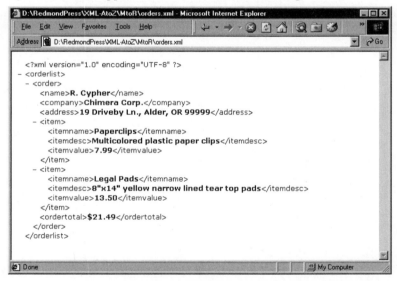

Figure P-2   A properly parsed XML document in Internet Explorer.

If you've chosen a document with a parsing error, it will appear similar to the document shown in Figure P-3.

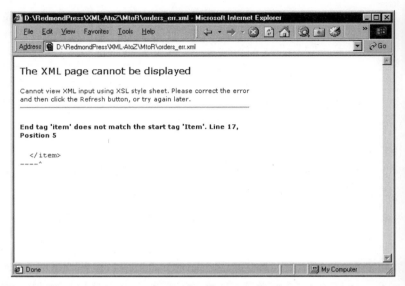

Figure P-3   A parsing error within Internet Explorer 5 stops the parsing of the document and displays the error.

Most parsers display a message informing you of the type and location of any errors that occur. If there were no errors in the document, then a parser not associated with a browser will return a message letting you know that your XML document is well-formed If the parser has a browser built-in, and the document has no errors, then the browser will typically display the contents of the XML document.

Online Parsers

There are a few nonvalidating XML parsers available online. These parsers view your document, either on your local machine or on another accessible Web server. They test it for well-formedness, but generally don't display the document itself. They typically only provide you with information about errors, when they occur.

NOTE   *If you are creating a lot of XML documents, download a local XML parser and use it for checking your documents to avoid overloading these free public use servers.*

- **RUWF (Are You Well-Formed).** This nonvalidating parser allows you to type in the address of any XML document accessible from the Internet. The RUWF site, found at *http://www.xml.com/pub/a/tools/ruwf/ check.html*, is shown in Figure P-4.

108

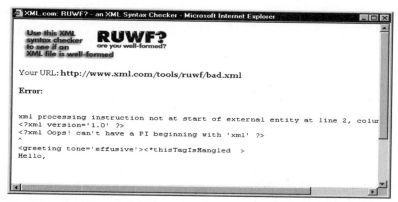

Figure P-4   The RUWF site results.

- **Frontier XML Syntax Checker.** This parser, shown in Figure P-5, is located at *http://frontier.userland.com/stories/storyReader$1092*. Frontier allows you to check any document located on the Internet with either the Frontier XML parser or the "blox" parser based upon the expat nonvalidating parser.

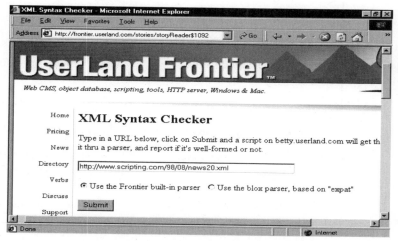

Figure P-5   The Frontier XML Syntax Checker Web site.

Validating Parsers

Validating parsers check the well-formedness of your document and verify that your document conforms to its specified Document Type Definition (DTD) or XML Schema. For checking a few documents, use one of the online XML validating parsers listed below. If you are creating a lot of documents, do the research and download (or purchase) a parser that works well for your applications.

- **Richard Tobins's well-formedness checker and validator.** Richard Tobins's validator is located at *http://www.cogsci.ed.ac.uk/~richard/xml-check.html*. This validator allows you to check any document on the Internet. To validate your XML documents with this parser, shown in Figure P-6, check the "validate?" box beneath the URL field on the Web page.

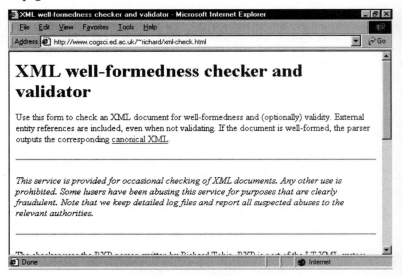

Figure P-6   Richard Tobins's well-formedness checker and validator.

- **The STG Validating Parser.** The STG parser is located at *http://www.stg.brown.edu/service/xmlvalid/* and shown in Figure P-7. It provides you a variety of options for checking pages, including Internet documents, text that you type into a form field, or a document located on your local computer.

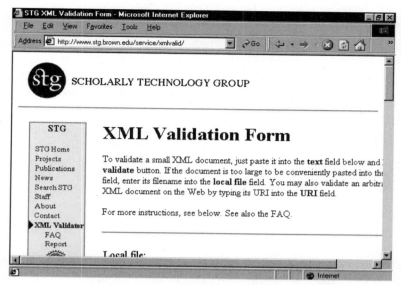

Figure P-7   The STG Validating Parser allows you to validate documents from practically anywhere.

SEE ALSO *Validating Documents, XML Software*

Perl

Perl is programming language that started in Unix machines and has since been ported to both Mac and Windows platforms. Perl is one of the most common languages for the development of CGI programs on Linux and Unix systems. Perl programs can work with HTML and XML documents, support Unicode, and can be used to interface with database programs such as Oracle, MySQL, and PostgreSQL. This language is flexible enough to support both object-oriented and procedural style programming while maintaining its open source (free) status and keeping the best parts of other programming languages, such as C, available. For more information on Perl, check out the Perl Monger's Web site located at *http://www.perl.org/press/ fast_facts.html*.

SEE ALSO *CGI*

Processing Applications see Parsers

Processing Instructions

Processing instructions (PI) allow you to incorporate proprietary application information into your XML document. In HTML, you had to use comment blocks and hope your application didn't ignore them.

PIs provide information that is only useable by the XML processor. This requires that the processor has been programmed to deal with the PI information, as well as restricting the format of the PI itself. Developers use PIs to share information about setting up document formats, control switch settings that the application requires to work with this document, or even run an external application.

PI Syntax

Processing instructions use the following notation:

```
<?pi_name pi_insruction?>
```

The pi_name provides a name for the instruction. In many cases, this is the name of the application that is processing the instruction or the name of the application that is used to display a file being referenced, as shown in the following examples:

```
<?realplayer presentation="myvideo.rm"?>

<?acrobat document="xml_specification.pdf"?>
```

The instruction itself can be composed of information identifying a file to load, a process to start, or even a switch to set when a program is started. Each of these scenarios is shown in the following examples:

```
<?realplayer load="myvideo.rm"?>

<?realplayer "play"?>

<?dos type "testing.txt" |more ?>
```

Because PIs are specific to the application that is processing your document, there are no formatting conventions that must be followed. The only restriction on the format of the PI is the format that can be used and read by the application doing the processing.

PIs can be used anywhere within your XML document after the opening <?xml?> declaration, which is also formatted like a processing instruction. The <?xml?> declaration actually is the processing instruction that lets the XML software know what kind of XML document it is loading and whether that document is a standalone file, or uses other files. You can use PIs to provide instructions within your document DTD or Schema, within the content of an element, or following the closing element of your XML document.

NOTE   *Processing instructions are not declared in the DTD or Schema. They are treated neither as elements, attributes, entities, or notations, and they are not treated as part of the structure of the XML document.*

Parsers do not process PIs—they strictly pass them on to the application that is ultimately using the XML document. The application determines how the PI is used.

PI Naming Rules and Restrictions

There are two restrictions on naming processing instructions:

• The name cannot start with xml. This string is reserved for the <?xml?> declaration, which is also a processing instruction.

• The name cannot start with or contain the ?> closing delimiter. This would close your processing instruction prior to the intended application processing the instructions.

The name of your processing instruction must follow the same set of rules that govern elements and attribute naming. The following PIs are used by XML application software to load the XML style sheet and explain the document encoding and version support level:

```
<?xml version="1.0" standalone="yes" encoding="Latin-1"?>

<?xml-stylesheet type="text/css" href="xml_spec.css"?>
```

PI Example

Because processing instructions (PI) formats are specific to the application they are intended for, every PI is different. A PI used to open a file in Windows Notepad could be formatted in the following fashion:

```
<?notepad myfile.txt?>
```

Processing instructions can include complex instructions controlling interactions with database applications whether retrieving, saving, or editing information found within the document.

In this example, the processing instruction <?SQL oracle8i.exe?> is used to inform an application what type of program should be used to read all instructions using the SQL designation:

```
<?xml version="1.0"?>

<!DOCTYPE  order [

    <!ELEMENT order ANY>
```

```
<!ELEMENT customer (name, address)>

<!ELMENT name (#PCDATA)>

<!ELEMENT address  (#PCDATA)>

]>

<?SQL oracle8i.exe?>

<order>

    <name> R. Cypher </name>

    <address> 444 Twisted St. Tacoma, WY 88888
    </address>

      <?SQL insert into Table1
values('#name','#address');?>

</order>
```

Prolog

In XML, the Prolog identifies the specification conformance level of the document being read. This statement enables document authors and future versions of user agents to take advantage of automatic version recognition. The prolog for a document that conforms to the XML 1.0 specification is as follows:

```
<?xml version="1.0" encoding="UTF-8"
standalone="no"?>
```

The prolog is developed by using the following construction code:

```
prolog ::=XMLDecl? Misc* (doctypedecl Misc*)?
```

XMLDecl

```
XMLDecl ::= '<?xml' VersionInfo EncodingDecl? SDDecl?
S? '?>'
```

The preceding statement lays out the main structure of the declaration and the order in which each of its individual parts must be implemented.

- VersionInfo ::= S 'version' Eq (' VersionNum' | " VersionNum")
  This specifies the version information with the string word version followed by the version number either in or out of quotation marks.

- Eq ::=S? '='S?   This inserts the equivalency sign into the version information. It can be either enclosed in quotes or not and should be followed by a string value.

- VersionNum ::= ([a-zA-Z0-9_.:] | '-')+   The version number is a string value containing any letters or numbers, a space, a period, a column, or a hyphen.

Misc

```
Misc ::= Comment | PI | S
```

This field contains a comment that can be used to provide extra information to the browser.

SEE ALSO *<?xml?>, Declarations, Processing Instructions*

Property

A property is any of the Cascading Style Sheet rules, or statements, that control the formatting of your XML documents.

SEE ALSO *Cascading Style Sheets*

Pseudo-Elements

Pseudo-elements are used in CSS to identify portions of an XML document not included as separate elements in the document source code. These type of elements represent abstractions in the XML document that there is no other way to identify, for instance, the first line of a paragraph. The following table lists the CSS Pseudo-elements:

PSEUDO-ELEMENT	DESCRIPTION
:after	Inserts information after the specified element.
:before	Inserts information before the specified element.
:first-child	Alters the properties of the first child element, of the specified element, no matter what the child is.
:first-letter	Alters the first letter of the contents of the specified element.
:first-line	Alters the first line of text in the contents of the specified element.
:lang	Specifies the language used for the specified element.

115

NOTE   *Web browsers prior to Netscape Navigator 6 and Internet Explorer 5 do not support most of these pseudo-elements, and even these browsers don't support them all.*

Public Identifiers

In the case of DTDs and Schemas, public identifiers point out the location of element and attribute definitions for use by the general public. In a DTD, a publicly available document declaration would appear as follows:

```
<!DOCTYPE root_element_name PUBLIC "DTD_name"
"DTD_URL">
```

SEE ALSO *<!DOCTYPE>, DTD*

RDF

RDF is an application of XML that enables structured metadata to be encoded, exchanged, and reused through multiple documents. The RDF framework allows the publication of both human-readable and machine-processable vocabularies describing the information contained within a XML application. The strict structure, imposed by RDF, uses standardized metadata systems, allowing the sharing of metadata by different industries and educational facilities. RDF has been used to implement site maps, set preferences for documents, provide collaborative services, and add information verification to e-commerce systems.

RDF provides the framework for standardizing metadata. The RDF data model does not declare the properties of metadata, nor does it define relationships between metadata properties and resources. RDF Schemas provide that functionality.

Using RDF you have instantaneous access to a globally supported method of sharing information about your XML documents. While metadata is typically customized to each document application, RDF specifies conventions that control how the semantics, syntax, and structure of metadata is formed.

Altogether you end up with a system, allowing you to merge metadata information from one industry into the information from a second industry and apply that merged data to a third industry without losing the capabilities of the original formats, only adding to their functionality.

116

NOTE   *RDF uses many of the ideas expressed in the Dublin Core for describing metadata. The Dublin Core metadata was designed to help researchers find electronic resources in a manner similar to using a library card catalog.*

RDF Basic Model

RDF uses multiple properties to describe each resource. Each property description is described by a statement with three parts: a property type, a value, and a resource. RDF can describe any resource with a unique URL.

The RDF model uses a namespace declaration to identify the document markup resources. The namespace for RDF is

```
<RDF xmlns="http://www.w3.org/TR/REC-rdf-syntax#">
```

By using namespaces, the RDF model allows you to access multiple resources, including the Dublin Core shown below:

```
<xmlns:DC="http://www.purl.org/DC#">
```

RDF Descriptors

An RDF description is composed of resources, properties, and statements.

Resources

An RDF resource could point to a complete document, such as *www.w3.org/index.htm*; parts of a document, such as a specific XML element; a database; or even an image. All resources must have uniquely identifiable URIs. Any object can have a URI, including sets of data that are yet to be created.

Properties

Properties are specific characteristics or attributes used to describe a resource. Properties have specific meanings identified by a value associated with the property's name, creating a name/value pair in the same fashion as CSS properties and XML attributes.

Statements

RDF statements are created by joining a property and its value for a specific resource. Statements are composed of the subject, the predicate, and the object. The subject represents the item being referenced, such as a person or a document. The predicate defines the role of the subject in reference to the resource. The object represents the value of the property as either another resource (URL) or a literal value.

117

RDF Basic Model Example

Take, for example, this statement:

```
Heather Williamson is the developer of http://
planetswissy.com/.
```

If you were to break this statement down into its component parts, you end up with a table of values similar to the following:

STATEMENT PART	VALUE
Subject (Resource)	*http://planetswissy.com/*
Predicate (Property)	Developer
Object(Literal)	Heather Williamson

This statement written in RDF would appear as follows:

```
<RDF xmlns="http://www.w3.org/TR/REC-rdf-syntax#">

  <DEVELOPER about="http://planetswissy.com/">

    Heather Williamson

  </DEVELOPER>

</RDF>
```

RDF Basic Syntax

The RDF specification allows two types of syntax for encoding a data model: serialization syntax and abbreviated syntax. Serialization syntax expresses data using elements, making the data visible on screen in XML-compliant applications. Abbreviated syntax uses attributes to provide a compact representation of the data.

NOTE   *RDF-compliant applications should be able to read both models of syntax, allowing you to use them together within a single RDF data block.*

Serialized RDF Syntax

Serialized statements use a series of "child elements," where the element contents represent the value of the property. The <rdf> tag is the opening and closing "root element" of the RDF resource, creating a boundary between the XML document and the content mapped to the RDF data model. The <description> element is the primary container for storing information about the RDF resource.

The basic RDF block using serialized syntax will look similar to the following code:

```
<rdf [namespacedeclaration(s)]>

  <rdf:description [id= name] | [about=URL]>

    <property> value </property>

    <!- Add as many properties as you have values
    for ->

    <property resourceAttr="URL" />

  </rdf:description>

</rdf>
```

NOTE   *The <RDF> element is not required, if it is obvious from the application context where the RDF block begins and ends.*

Serialized RDF Syntax Example

In this example, a simple RDF block identifies the document address (*www.planetswissy.com*) and the name of the developer (Heather Williamson).

```
Heather Williamson developed the document located at
http://www.planetswissy.com.

<rdf xmlns="http://www.w3.org/TR/REC-rdf-syntax#">

  <description >

    <about>http://www.planetswissy.com/</about>

    <developer>Heather Williamson</developer>

  </description>

</rdf>
```

This example uses a more complicated joining of structures from both the RDF schematic or the Dublin Core.

```
Heather Williamson, created the "The Planet Swissy
Web Page" located at http://www.planetswissy.com/
index.html, whose contact email address is
webmaster@planetswissy.com, on January 1, 2002.

<rdf xmlns="http://www.w3.org/TR/REC-rdf-syntax#"

      xmlns:DC="http://www.purl.org/DC#">

  <description>
```

```
<DC:ABOUT>http://www.planetswissy.com/</DC:ABOUT>

<DC:CREATOR> Heather Williamson </DC:CREATOR >

<DC:TITLE> The Planet Swissy Web Site </DC:TITLE>

<DC:CONTACT> webmaster@planetswissy.com
  </DC:CONTACT>

<DC:DATE> January 1, 2002</DC:DATE>

</description>

</rdf>
```

Abbreviated RDF Syntax

Abbreviated syntax is less clear to read for people than serialized syntax. Although not as popular, it does provide RDF data in a compact format, using abbreviated RDF syntax documents with well-structured XML DTDs or Schemas to be directly read as RDF models.

The primary form of an abbreviated syntax uses unique properties/attributes within the Description element to define the RDF information. This basic syntax is shown in the following example:

```
<df [namespacedeclaration(s)]>

  <rdf:description [id= name] | [about=URL]

      property1=value

      property2=value

      property3=value .../>

</rdf>
```

NOTE   *Because the <description> element no longer has child elements, it is written using the syntax of an empty element.*

Abbreviated RDF Syntax Example

Using abbreviated syntax, the following statement would be written as follows:

```
Heather Williamson developed the document located at
http://www.planetswissy.com.

<rdf xmlns="http://www.w3.org/TR/REC-rdf-syntax#">

  <description about="http://www.planetswissy.com/"

    developer="Heather Williamson" />
```

120

```
</rdf>
```

More complex statements can be expressed in abbreviated format, as shown in the following RDF example:

```
Heather Williamson, created the "The Planet Swissy
Web Page" located at http://www.planetswissy.com/
index.html, whose contact email address is
webmaster@planetswissy.com, on January 1, 2002.

<rdf xmlns="http://www.w3.org/TR/REC-rdf-syntax#"

    xmlns:DC="http://www.purl.org/DC#>

  <description about="http://www.planetswissy.com/"

    DC:CREATOR="Heather Williamson"

    DC:TITLE="The Planet Swissy Web Pages "

    DC:CONTACT="webmaster@planetswissy.com"

    DC:DATE=" January 2, 2002" />

</rdf>
```

RDF Schema

The Resource Description Framework (RDF) Schema allows for the exchange of computer-readable descriptions of Internet resources. RDF Schema provides a means of processing metadata about XML documents. This schema is based on XML. Using XML, RDF Schemas exchange information about resources, whether the resource is an XML document or a Java application. RDF Schema uses include sharing information about resources with search engines and creating catalogs of Web site documents, or they can be used as a document rating system.

NOTE   *The Resource Description Framework Schema is available from the Web Consortium Web site located at* http://www.w3.org/RDF/.

RDF Schema, unlike the original RDF specification, provides a means of describing the data sets used. Using the Schema, you can declare the document structure of the properties being tracked as metadata. Schemas define the properties of a resource, including title, author, and resource types, such as books, e-mail messages, presentations, or streaming video.

Unlike DTDs and XML Schemas, an RDF Schema describes how the metadata information is interpreted, not how the document is put together.

The RDF Schema performs the following tasks:

- Identifies the mechanisms needed to define elements as metadata
- Defines the classes of resources which may use a specific element
- Restricts the number of possible combinations of classes and relationships
- Detects any violations of its specified restrictions

Simply, the RDF Schema defines a metadata specification language.

SEE ALSO   *RDF, XML Applications*

Recursion

Recursion, in the terms of an XML document, is the use of an element as a child of itself. For instance, the following document would use recursion of the <order> element:

```
<order>

  <order>

  </order>

</order>
```

In a DTD, this document would be described as

```
<!ELEMENT order (order)>
```

Notably, this is an impractical use of the element, and it wouldn't be difficult to give one of the order elements a new name, such as orderlist or purchaseorder, to more concretely identify the meaning of the element in its applied context.

Redundancy

Redundant information is sometimes good and sometimes bad. Having a redundant backup system is often a lifesaver, but in databases, you don't want redundant information in the same document source. Redundant information in databases creates two or more locations for you to enter data, which can then be inadvertently altered in such a way that two records no longer contain the exact same information.

In XML documents, redundancy may be necessary, although with proper document organization much of the redundancy can be removed. Through the application of XSLT you can alter the order of elements, and reuse their content, so you don't need to implement redundant statements, as may be necessary with CSS.

SEE ALSO *Database*

Resource Description Framework see RDF

Root Elements

XML documents have a single root element that must serve as the all-inclusive base for the rest of the document. This root element, similar to the <html> element in HTML documents, provides your document's foundation. But with XML you get to identify the name of the element. In other words, if you are identifying the contents of a business purchase order, your root element could be <order>. If you are identifying the content of a project tracking system, your root element might be <projects>.

Schemas

XML Schemas allow you to create rules that control the validity of XML documents. Schemas are used to define the structure, content, and semantics of XML documents for use with validating parsers.

XML Schemas derive from XML, so like XML they can be written in a simple text editor or through one of the available Schema editors downloadable from the Internet.

NOTE   *Schemas will change as XML and its subsidiary languages change. The World Wide Web Consortium at* http://www.w3.org/ TR/xml/ *keeps track of the Schema specification. Articles on XML Schemas are available at the XMLHack site located at* http:// www.xmlhack.com *as well as the XML.com site, located at* http://www.xml.com.

Schema Specifications

XML Schemas provide more control over your XML documents than is available with DTDs. Schemas work with both XML documents and XML Namespaces. They can be applied to XML documents to constrain it, much the same way as a DTD, but with these considerations:

- Schemas are more expressive than XML DTDs.
- Schemas are expressed in XML.
- Schemas are usable by most applications that employ XML.
- Schemas are usable on the Internet.
- Schemas are optimized for interoperability.
- Schemas are simple to implement using the design of an XML document.

- Schemas are coordinated with related World Wide Web Consortium specifications, including XML Information Set, XLink, XML Namespaces, XPointers, style sheets recommendations, the Document Object Model, and the Resource Description Framework Schema.

NOTE   *Information on the three documents comprising the XML Schema is in the following documents:* http://www.w3.org/TR/xmlschema-0/, http://www.w3.org/TR/xmlschema-1/, *and* http://www.w3.org/TR/xmlschema-2/.

Schema Definition Language

XML Schema Definition Language (XSD) is a powerful but flexible document definition language providing controls over the existence of elements and attributes, document content, and element order. It also specifies data types, when and where elements and attributes can be used, and the content of attributes. Validating parsers use schemas to test the information in a document after parsing is complete. Parsing includes the expansion of entities and the loading of default attribute values. When using a Schema to evaluate an XML document, a list of violations of the Schema constraints, as well as the resulting enhanced information set, will be returned to you.

The following table shows how XML Schemas work with XML document markup objects:

XML OBJECTS	SCHEMA INTERACTIONS
Elements	Schemas control how elements can be used by identifying which elements are constrained by using complex types to control element content.
Element content	Schemas control which values are allowed in the element based on the current element type and its ancestor types.
Attributes	Schemas control attributes by associating them with elements and restraining them using constraints.
Attribute values	Schemas control attribute values using data types and regular expressions.
Entities	Entities are not constrained by Schemas.
Notations	Notations are not constrained by Schemas.

XML OBJECTS	SCHEMA INTERACTIONS
Comments	Comments are not constrained by Schemas.
Processing	PIs are not constrained by Schemas.
`<?xml ?>`	The XML declaration is a processing instruction and therefore not constrained.
XML namespaces	Namespaces are not constrained by Schemas.

Comparing DTDs and Schemas

DTDs focus on providing simple datatyping of attributes and elements. XML Schemas provide systematic datatyping using complex datatypes. XML DTDs provide a basic macro functionality, using parameter entities, while schemas allow you to re-create these functions using the built-in features listed in the following table:

DTD FEATURE	SCHEMA FEATURE
DOCTYPE	Schemas have no equivalent because they do not use the "document" concept. Schemas work with elements and attributes contained in namespaces or XML documents.
Internal and external subset	There is no equivalent declaration with schemas. Schemas contained in the XML document use `<include>`, `<import>`, and `<redefine>` to work with Schemas that are not included in the XML document.
ELEMENT	`<xsd:element>`
#PCDATA element content	`<xsd:element mixed=true>`
ANY element content	`<any>` or `<anyAttribute>`
EMPTY element content	`<xsd:complexType mixed="false">`
Content Model	`<xsd:complexType>`
, (Sequence Connector)	`<xsd:sequence>`

DTD FEATURE	SCHEMA FEATURE
| (Alternative Connector)	`<xsd:choice>`
? (Optional)	`<xsd:element minOccurs="x">` and `<xsd:element maxOccurs="x">`
+ (required and repeatable)	`<xsd:element minOccurs="x">` and `<xsd:element maxOccurs="x">`
* (optional and repeatable)	`<xsd:element minOccurs="x">` and `<xsd:element maxOccurs="x">`
( ) (groups)	`<xsd:group>`
ATTLIST	`<xsd:attribute>` and grouped with `<attributeGroup>`
Multiple ATTLIST declarations	`<xsd:attribute>` contains only one attribute. Multiple attributes are grouped, although not defined using `<attributegroup>`.
CDATA attribute type	Use a built-in simple type or a pattern attribute using regular expressions.
ID attribute type	Use a simple type, plus `<xsd:unique>`.
IDREF IDREFS attribute types	Use the simple type, in addition to the `<key>` and `<keyref>` elements.
NOTATION attribute type	Use a simple type with a pattern attribute.
NMTOKEN NMTOKENS attribute types	Use a simple type with a pattern attribute.

DTD FEATURE	SCHEMA FEATURE
ENTITY ENTITIES attribute types Instructions (PIs)	Use a simple type with a pattern attribute containing regular expressions.
Enumerations	Use a simple type.
Attribute defaults	<xsd:attribute use="default">
#FIXED attributes	<xsd:attribute use="default">
#REQUIRED and #IMPLIED	use="prohibited", use="optional", or use="required" attributes.
ENTITY	Use either a simple or fixed type.
ENTITY % Parameter entity declaration	Use <attributeGroup> or a named <complexType>.
IGNORE/INCLUDE marked sections	Not supported
NOTATION Declaration	Use a simple type, or the standard Notation syntax..
Comments in DTDs	XML <documentation> child element of the <annotation> element provides comments.
Processing instructions	<appinfo> child element of the <annotation> element provides Processing Instruction (PI) functionality; although traditional DTD-formatted PIs can still be used.

NOTE   *Parameter entities are supported in schemas using the following functions:*

- *<complexType>*
- *<attributeGroup>*
- *Datatypes and Regular Expressions*
- *<import> , <include> and <redefine>*

127

Schema Annotations

Schemas use the <annotation> element to provide comments accessible by the XML Parser or browser. Standard comment statements, formatted the same for both DTDs and Schemas, only provide information to people reading a document.

XML Schema uses three elements for annotating Schemas: annotation, documentation, and appInfo.

- **annotation** Parent element for both the documentation and appInfo elements.

- **documentation** Provides comments, such as a description of the Schema and its copyright information, for people to read.

- **appInfo** Provides information on style sheets, tools, and other application-specific information for your XML application software.

The following example shows how you can use the annotation element to provide information for both people and applications using the <documentation> and <appInfo> tags. The following example provides a description for a Schema describing an invoice and its style sheet:

```
<xsd:schema>

  <xsd:annotation>

    <xsd:documentation>

      Schema document describing the format of
      purchase orders for Williamson Office
      Supplies.

    </xsd:documentation>

    <xsd:documentation>

      Copyright (c) 2002 Williamson Inc. All rights
      reserved.

    </xsd:documentation>

    <xsd:appInfo source="http://www.mystore.com/
    stylesheet.css">

      Download CSS style sheet

    </xsd:appInfo>

  </xsd:annotation>

</xsd:schema>
```

128

Schema Constraints

<complexTypes> of elements typically require the addition of constraints to your statements. Element constraints control the occurrence of elements, or element groups, within the XML document.

The three primary constraints used on groups of elements are as follows:

- **<choice>** Only one of the elements listed may appear in that document location.

- **<sequence>** Elements must appear in the same order (sequence) as declared.

- **<all>** Elements occur in any order and in any combination.

NOTE   *Each of these constraints can use the minOccurs and maxOccurs attributes to further restrict the use of each element.*

<choice>

The <choice> constraint describes a choice between several possible elements or element groups. Your XML document can contain only one of these choices. The basic structure of a <choice> constraint is shown in the following code:

```
<xsd:complexType>

   <xsd:choice>

      <xsd:element name="element1" .../>

      <xsd:element name="element2" .../>

      <xsd:element name="element3" .../>

      <xsd:element name="element4" .../>

   </xsd:choice>

</xsd:complexType>
```

This code enforces the rule that the XML document can use only one of these elements.

You can also force a choice between groups of elements, as shown in the following code example:

```
<xsd:complexType>

   <xsd:choice>

      <xsd:element ref="group1" />
```

129

```
        <xsd:element ref="group2" />

        <xsd:element ref="group3" />

    </xsd:choice>

</xsd:complexType>
```

NOTE   *Each of the groups used in a <choice> statement must be defined in the Schema document prior to the <choice> constraint.*

<sequence>

The <sequence> constraint forces an order to your elements. In other words, the order of element declarations in your XML document must match the order in which elements were specified in the schema. A sample sequence is shown below:

```
<xsd:complexType>

    <xsd:sequence>

        <xsd:element name="element1" />

        <xsd:element name="element2" />

        <xsd:element name="element3" />

    </xsd:sequence>

</xsd:complexType>
```

Control the sequence of element groups using the following notation:

```
<xsd:complexType>

    <xsd:sequence>

        <xsd:element ref="group1" />

        <xsd:element ref="group2" />

        <xsd:element ref="group3" />

    </xsd:sequence>

<xsd:complexType>
```

<all>

<all> defines an unordered set of elements, allowing any element in the group to appear once or not at all, in any order. <all> can only be used on the top level of a content model. When used with groups, the child elements cannot be complexType elements and can appear just once in the document.

The following complexType definition allows the elements described to appear in any order:

```
<xsd:complexType name="invoiceLineItem">

  <xsd:all>

   <xsd:element name="element1"/>

   <xsd:element name="element2"/>

   <xsd:element name="element3">

  </xsd:all>

 </xsd:complexType>
```

Multiple Constraints

Constraints can be combined to create more complex sets of criteria for your document. Constraints can be used inside groups, complex types, or other constraints. For instance, the following example will accept either a single "address" element or a sequence of "billingaddress", a "shippingaddress", and an optional "billingemail" element:

```
<xsd:group name="orderaddress">

  <xsd:choice>

   <xsd:element name="address" type="xsd:string" />

   <xsd:sequence>

    <xsd:element name="billingaddress"
    type="xsd:string" />

    <xsd:element name="shippingaddress"
    type="xsd:string" />

    <xsd:element name="billingemail"
    type="xsd:string" minOccurs="0"/>

   </xsd:sequence>

  </xsd:choice>

 </xsd:group>
```

Constraint Restrictions on <all>

In order to avoid combinations that could become ambiguous or too complex to be solved by W3C XML Schema tools, a set of restrictions has been added to the <all> constraint:

- <all> can appear only as a unique child at the top of a content model.

131

- <all> can contain only simple <element> definitions, which occur no more than once.

Schema Data Types

Schemas break XML document element content down into two main types: simple and complex. Complex types can use a combination of element and text content as well as attributes, while simple types can have neither child elements nor attributes.

Complex Types

Complex types of elements allow attributes and elements as content using the <complexType> Schema element declaration. This declaration is contained within the <element> Schema declaration, which names the complex element, as you can see in the following code:

```
<xsd:element name="order">

  <xsd:complexType>

  </xsd:complexType>

</xsd:element>
```

Complex Type Example

The following example uses <complexType> to define the elements and attributes, using <attribute>, contained within a purchase order record:

```
<xsd:element name="purchaseorder">

  <xsd:complexType>

   <xsd:sequence>

    <xsd:element name="name">

     <xsd:complexType>

      <xsd:sequence>

       <xsd:element name="firstname"
       type="xsd:string" />

       <xsd:element name="lastname"
       type="xsd:string" />

      </xsd:sequence>

      <xsd:attribute name="custid"
      type="xsd:string" />
```

```
      </xsd:complexType>

    </xsd:element>

    <xsd:element name="address" type="xsd:string" />

    <xsd:element name="city" type="xsd:string" />

    <xsd:element name="state" type="xsd:string" />

    <xsd:element name="zip" type="xsd:decimal" />

    </xsd:sequence>

  </xsd:complexType>

</xsd:element>
```

The preceding code forces any element that has been named "purchaseorder" to contain in order a <name> element composed of a <firstname> and <lastname> element and a "custid" attribute, as well as <address>, <city>, <state>, and <zip> elements.

Creating Your Own Complex Type

You could also have defined a complexType named "purchaseorder" that works like a DTD NMTOKEN so that you can apply the type "purchaseorder" to any element and have that element take on the definition of the "purchaseorder", including all of its child elements and attributes.

```
<xsd:complexType name="purchaseorder">

  <xsd:sequence>

    ... element declarations for the purchase order...

  </xsd:sequence>

</xsd:complexType>
```

To create an element of complexType "purchaseorder", you simply need to create an element of type="purchaseorder", as shown in the following statement:

```
<element name="address" type="ContactRecord" />
```

When defining elements and complexTypes, you can't have two elements with the same name, but you can have an element and a complexType with the same name You can't have both a simpleType and a complexType with the same name. You can have two elements with the same name as long as they are parts of different complex types. If you break any of these rules, a parsing error will occur.

Simple Types

XML Schemas define multiple simple types enabling you to control the type of content used within elements and attributes. The following table lists the simple types included in the XML Schema specification:

TYPE	EXAMPLE	USE
Binary	#99FFCC	Binary data in either Hex or Base-64 notation.
Boolean	false	Either true or false.
Byte	-23 , 126, 0	Represents an integer between -128 and 127.
CDATA	"my string"	A white-spaced normal ized strings without a carriage-return (#xD), line-feed (#xA), or tab (#x9) character.
Century	21	Gregorian calendar specification for a day.
Date	2002-09-19	Gregorian calendar specification for a day.
Decimal	-10.34, -1.56, 0.23, 2.9	Arbitrary precision decimal number.
Double	-INF, -1E4, -0, 0, 12.78E-2, 12, INF, NaN	Double-precision 64-bit floating-point type number whose absolute value is less than 2^{53}, and e is an integer between 1075 and 970, inclusive.
ENTITIES	<	A space-separated list of ENTITY items.
ENTITY	&	An XML 1.0 ENTITY attribute type.

TYPE	EXAMPLE	USE
Float	-INF, -1E4, -0, 0, 12.78E-2, INF, NaN	Single-precision 32-bit floating point. NaN stands for "not a number."
ID	row2col10	XML 1.0 ID attribute type.
IDREF	item="row2col10"	XML 1.0 IDREF attribute type.
IDREFS	row2col10, pg10	A space-separated list of IDREF items.
Int	—2147483648 to 2147483647	Integer.
Integer	-126789 to 126789	Any whole number.
Language	en-gb, fr	Any valid value for the xml:lang attribute as defined in XML 1.0.
Long	-922337203 6854775808 to 9223372 036854775807	Long integer.
Month	2005-07	Gregorian calendar specification for a month.
Name	Any string of characters	Any XML valid name.
NCName	Any string of characters other than the colon	"Non-colonized" XML names.
NegativeInteger	-126789 to −1	Integer value below 0.
NMTOKEN	Any name token valid in XML 1.0	XML 1.0 NMTOKEN attribute type.
NMTOKENS	Any name token valid in XML 1.0	A space-separated list of NMTOKEN items.

TYPE	EXAMPLE	USE
NonNegativeInteger	0 to 126789	Integer value 0 or greater.
NonPositiveInteger	-126789 to 0	Integer value greater than 0 or less.
NOTATION	XML compliant character string	XML 1.0 NOTATION attribute type.
PositiveInteger	1 to 126789	Positive integer greater than 1.
Qname	XML compliant character string	Namespace-qualified, XML-compliant name.
RecurringDate	—07-31	A recurring day of the year, such as the thirty-first of July.
RecurringDay	——31	A recurring day of the month, such as the 31st of the month.
RecurringDuration	—05-31T 13:20:00	A period of time recurring at a specified frequency.
Short	-32768 to 32767	Short integer value.
String	string of characters	The ASCII character set.
Time	13:20:00.000, 13:20:00.000-05:00	An instant of time.
TimeDuration	P1Y2M3D T10H30M12.3S	A specific duration of time.

TYPE	EXAMPLE	USE
TimeInstant	2005-07-31T 13:20:00.000 -08:00	A specific instant in time on the Gregorian calendar, for example, July 31st, 2005, at 1:20 P.M. Pacific Standard Time, which is 8 hours behind Coordinated Universal Time (UTC).
TimePeriod	2005-07-31T13:20	A specific period of time with a specified start and end.
Token	All character data	A set of strings that do not contain the line-feed (#xA), tab (#x9) characters, leading or trailing spaces (#x20), or internal sequences of two or more spaces.
UnsignedByte	0 to 255	Positive integer value.
UnsignedInt	0 to 4294967295	Positive integer value.
UnsignedLong	0 to 18446744 073709551615	Positive integer value.
UnsignedShort	0 to 65535	Positive integer value.
UriReference	http://www. mysite.com	Any Internet or intranet address.
Year	2005	Gregorian calendar year.

Schema Definition Language Attributes

XML documents use attributes to further define elements in XML documents. XML Schemas use attributes to provide specific information about the elements and attributes being defined by the Schema. The following table lists the Schema attributes used in the description of the contents of the XML document.

ATTRIBUTE	VALUES AND DESCRIPTION
Abstract	true | false Forces the creation of an abstract element or attribute.
AttributeForm Default	unqualified | qualified Indicates the form of locally declared attributes.
Base	simple type Indicates the base type of an element or attribute.
Block	restrictions | #all | extensions Blocks specific types of elements or attributes from use within an element.
BlockDefault Default	restrictions | #all | extensions Essentially specifies a block attribute on every element declaration.
ElementForm	unqualified | qualified Indicates the form of a locally declared element.
Final	restrictions | #all | extensions Blocks specific types of elements or attributes from use within an element.
FinalDefault	restrictions | #all | extensions Essentially specifies a final attribute on every and element declaration.
Fixed	true | false Prevents facets from being modified.
Form	unqualified | qualified Controls element qualifications.

ATTRIBUTE	VALUES AND DESCRIPTION
ItemType	A type reference for a previously created type Uses a custom type, or simple type, to create a new item.
MemberTypes	A type reference for a previously created type A list of types in the <union> element.
MaxOccurs	nonNegativeInteger | unbounded Maximum number of times an element can occur.
MinOccurs	nonNegativeInteger | unbounded Minimum number of times an element may appear.
Mixed	true | false Allows mixed content in an element.
Name	text string Identifies the reference name of an object.
Namespace	##any | ##local | ##other | "URI" Identifies the namespace of an element.
NoNameSpace Location	http://www.w3.org/2000/10/XMLSchema-instance Provides the locations of Schema documents without target namespaces.
xsi:null	true | false Applies a null value for the element inside the XML document.
Nullable	true | false Allows an XML element to be null in an XML document.
ProcessContents	strict | lax Controls how strict the validation process is.
Ref	The name of a previously defined element References an existing named element.
SchemaLocation	URL Contains the namespace and appropriate Schema document.

ATTRIBUTE	VALUES AND DESCRIPTION
xsi:schema Location	URL Provides the address for a Schema document.
SubstitutionGroup	Name of existing group Specifies a group of elements used to replace another element.
TargetNamespace	URL Identifies the target document's namespace.
Type	A simple type or a custom type identifier Identifies an object's content type.
xsi:type	A simple type or a custom type identifier Identifies an object's content type.
Use	prohibited | optional | required | default | fixed Indicates how an attribute is used.
Value	string Provides a value for an attribute.
Xpath	An XPath expression Provides an XPath expression for locating an attribute's destination resource.

NOTE   *Check with the latest Schema recommendation located at* http://www.w3.org/XML/Schemas *for the most current information on these attributes.*

Schema Definition Language Elements

XML Schemas use predefined elements to specify the rules controlling the organization of XML documents. When contained in your XML document, schema elements must start with the prefix xsd:, identifying the Schema Namespace declared as xmlns:xsd="http://www.w3.org/2000/10/XMLSchema". Apply this namespace declaration to the root <schema> element, and use it throughout the Schema to identify the Schema elements and attributes separate from the XML document elements and attributes.

The xsd: prefix must also be applied to simple types. The prefix associates with a specified type as one of the predefined types in the XML Schema language, rather than associating them with a vocabulary created within the document. Although the xsd: prefix is not required in separate Schema documents, I suggest using it for readability.

NOTE   *Read the XML Schema recommendation at the World Wide Web Consortium (W3C) Web site at* http://www.w3.org/XML/Schemas *for the latest schema language development information.*

Schema documents use XML document structure, so you don't have to learn new formats, just the elements, their attributes, and the syntax for Schemas. The elements, which are described in the following table:

ELEMENT	SYNTAX AND DESCRIPTION
All	`<all id="ID"  maxOccurs="1:1" minOccurs="1:1"...> (annotation? , element*) </all>` Allows elements to appear in any order.
Annotation	`<annotation>(appinfo | documentation)*</annotation>` Creates comments
Any	`<any id="ID" minOccurs="0|Unbounded" maxOccurs="1" namespace="namespace" ...> (annotation?) </any>` Represents a wild card element.
AnyAttribute	`<anyAttribute id="ID" namespace="namespace" processContents = (skip | lax | strict)...> (annotation?) </anyAttribute>` Represents a wild card attribute inside an elements.
AppInfo	`<appInfo source=URI> ({any})* </appInfo>` Provides comments/information for the application.
Attribute	`<attribute  form = (qualified | unqualified) id = ID name = NCName  ref = QName ype = QName  use = (prohibited | optional | required | default | fixed)   value = string. ..>(annotation? , (simpleType?))</attribute>` Creates an attribute for a `<complexType>` element.
AttributeGroup	`<attributeGroup  id = ID  ref = QName  ...>(annotation?)</attributeGroup>` Creates a group of attributes.

ELEMENT	SYNTAX AND DESCRIPTION
Choice	<choice id="ID" minOccurs="0:Unbounded" maxOccurs="0:1" ...> (annotation? , (element | group | choice | sequence | any)*) </choice> Forces a choice to be made between offered elements.
ComplexContent	<complexContent id = ID mixed = boolean . . .>(annotation? , (restriction | extension)) </complexContent> Creates a mixed content element.
ComplexType	<complexType abstract = boolean block = (#all | List of (extension | restriction)) final = (#all | List of (extension | restriction)) id = ID mixed = boolean name = NCName . . .> (annotation? , simpleContent | complexContent | ((group | all | choice | sequence)? , ((attribute | attributeGroup)* , anyAttribute?)))) </complexType> Creates an element allowing child elements and attributes in addition to text content.
Documentation	<documentation source=URI xml:lang=language> ({any})* </documentation> Documents the schema document.
Element	<element abstract = boolean block = (#all | List of (substitution | extension | restriction)) default = string final = (#all | List of (extension | restriction)) fixed = string form = (qualified | unqualified) id = ID maxOccurs = (nonNegativeInteger | unbounded) minOccurs = nonNegativeInteger name = NCName nullable = boolean ref = QName substitutionGroup = QName type = QName . . . > (annotation? , ((simpleType | complexType)? , (key | keyref | unique)*)) </element> Creates an element.

ELEMENT	SYNTAX AND DESCRIPTION
Extension	`<extension base = QName id = ID . . .>` (annotation? , ((attribute | attributeGroup)* , anyAttribute?))`</extension>` Creates attributes for elements with `<complexContent>`.
Field	`<field id = ID xpath = An XPath expression . . .>`(annotation?)`</field>` Creates an XPath field.
Group	`<group id = ID maxOccurs =` (nonNegativeInteger | unbounded)minOccurs = onNegativeInteger name = NCName ref = QName . . .>(annotation? , (all | choice | sequence)?) `</group>` Creates groups of elements.
Import	`<import id = ID namespace = URI schemalocation=URI. . >`(annotation?)`</import>` Identifies a namespace and associates it with a Schema.
Include	`<include id = ID schemalocation=URI. . >`(annotation?)`</include>` Incorporates the content contained in another Schema file, into the current Schema.
Key	`<key id = ID   name = NCName . . >`(annotation? , (selector , field+))`</key>` Forces the values of designated elements to be unique and not nullable.
KeyRef	`<keyRef id = ID name = NCName refer=QName. . >`(annotation? , (selector , field+))`</keyRef>` References a key element.
List	`<list id = ID itemtype=QName. . >`(annotation? , (simpletype?))`</list>` Creates a new list type by deriving it from an existing atomic types.

ELEMENT	SYNTAX AND DESCRIPTION
Notation	<notation id = ID name = NCName public = PUBLIC_identifier system = uriReference. . >(annotation?) </notation> Creates the Schema version of an XML DTD NOTATION.
Pattern	<pattern value = string /> Provides a pattern using regular expressions that must be matched using the <restriction> element.
Redefine	<redefine schemaLocation = uriReference. . >(annotation | (attributeGroup | complexType | group | simpleType))*</redefine> Allows the redefinition of simple and complex types, groups, and attribute groups obtained from external Schema files.
Restriction	<restriction base = QName id = ID ...>(annotation? , (simpleType? , (duration | encoding | enumeration | length | maxExclusive | maxInclusive | maxLength | minExclusive | minInclusive | minLength | pattern | period | precision | scale | whiteSpace)*)? , ((attribute | attributeGroup)* , anyAttribute?)) </restriction> Indicates the existing (base) type and facets that constrain the range of values.
Schema	<schema attributeFormDefault = (qualified | unqualified) blockDefault = (#all | List of (substitution | extension | restriction)) elementFormDefault = (qualified | unqualified) finalDefault = (#all | List of (extension | restriction)) id = ID targetNamespace = uriReference version = string . . .>((include | import | redefine | annotation)* , ((attribute | attributeGroup | complexType | element | group | notation | simpleType) , annotation*)*)</schema> The root element of an XML Schema document required at the opening and closing of every Schema.

ELEMENT	SYNTAX AND DESCRIPTION
Selector	<selector id = ID xpath = An XPath expression . . .>(annotation?)</selector> Selects all elements meeting specific criteria. Works with the <field> element.
Sequence	<sequence id="ID" minOccurs="0:Unbounded" maxOccurs="0:1" ...>(annotation? , (element | group | choice | sequence | any)*)</sequence> Forces the elements in the content of the XML document to appear in a specific order.
SimpleContent	<simpleContent id = ID . . .>(annotation? , (restriction | extension))</simpleContent> Creates a type containing only character data.
SimpleType	<simpleType id = ID name = NCName . . .>(annotation? , ((list | restriction | union)))</simpleType> Defines and names a new simple type.
Union	<union id = ID membertypes=Qname List. . >(annotation? , (simpletype?))</union> Enables an element or attribute value drawn from the union of multiple list types.
Unique	<unique id = ID name = NCName . . >(annotation? , (selector , field+))</unique> Requires that a specified attribute or element value is unique.

Schema Editors

Editors for Schemas are much the same as other document editors. Some allow you to convert DTDs into Schemas; an increasingly important feature as XML Schemas take over the work of defining XML documents.

XML Spy

XML Spy, available from *http://www.xmlspy.com*, supports both editing and validation of

- XML Schema Definition (XSD)
- Document Type Definitions (DTDs)
- Document Content Descriptions (DCDs)

XML Spy, shown in Figure S-1, validates your XML document against all of the primary Schema types or creates a Schema from an XML document.

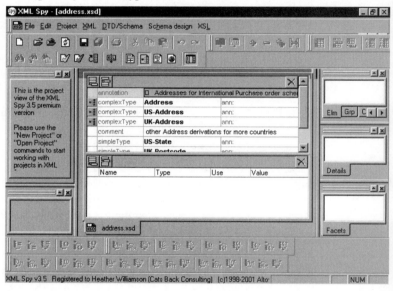

Figure S-1   XML Spy allows direct editing of your Schema.

Turbo XML

Turbo XML, shown in Figure S-2, available from Tibco Extensibility at *http://www.extensibility.com*, has combined three pieces of software focused on creating XML documents, Schemas, and DTDs while simultaneously validating and parsing those documents to ensure that they are well-formed.

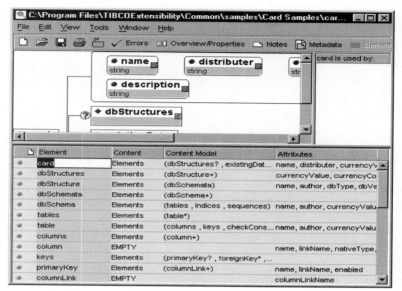

Figure S-2   Turbo XML creates Schemas, XML documents, and DTDs.

Turbo XML includes the following individual programs:

- XML Authority creates, converts, and manages DTDs and XML Schemas.

- XML Instance provides a development environment for the creation, editing, and management of XML documents and related files.

- XML Console provides a centralized documentation management, validation, and conversion location over a network.

Schema Element Content

Using XML Schemas, you can define elements with both element content and text content, as well as define attributes with mixed content (attributes, child elements, and text). You can create multiple variations on the makeup of element content, some of which are discussed below.

Attributes and Simple Values

Assigning both an attribute value and a simple value to your elements is quite easy. Take, for instance, the following <name> element. It uses an attribute to provide salutation information and simple string content to provide the actual name of the person being discussed:

147

```
<name salutation="Mr."> Tony Lion </name>
```

To define this element in your Schema, start with the basic name element, as shown in the following statement:

```
<xsd:element name="name" type="xsd:string" />
```

To expand this element, convert the simple type into a complex type, as shown in the following example code:

```
<xsd:element name="name">

<xsd:complexType>

 <xsd:simpleContent>

  <xsd:extension base="xsd:string">

   <xsd:attribute name="salutation"
   type="xsd:string" />

  </xsd:extension>

 </xsd:simpleContent>

</xsd:complexType>

</xsd:element>
```

In this example, the <complexType> element created a new anonymous type definition, which was modified by the <simpleContent> element. The <simpleContent> statement indicates that the content model of the new type contains only character data. The <extension> element expands the original string type by enabling a standard <attribute> declaration statement that is used to define the salutation used with this contact.

Mixed Content

When needing both character and element content within your elements, you must create a mixed content element. The Schema statements must provide both element and character content for your customer element, as shown below:

```
<customer>

  R. Cypher

 <company> Willards Sales and Service </company>

 <address> 444 Tigard Way, Tualitin, WY 88888
 </address>

</customer>
```

The following XML Schema defines the company element with character content and two child elements, <company> and <address>:

```
<xsd:element name="customer">
  <xsd:complexType mixed="true">
    <xsd:sequence>
      <xsd:element name="company" type="xsd:string" />
      <xsd:element name="address" type="xsd:string"/>
    </xsd:sequence>
  </xsd:complexType>
</xsd:element>
```

Empty Content

An element with only attributes is described using a <complexType> statement with no specified child elements. Take for instance a company contact record where all information is stored within attributes of the element itself, as shown in the following XML element statement:

```
<company name="Willards Sales and Service"
         owner="R. Cypher"
         address="Tualatin, WY" />
```

To restrict this element to no content, define an element with attributes and declare any elements within its content. This setup, as shown in the following code, forces the element's content model to be empty other than any applied attributes:

```
<xsd:element name="company">
  <xsd:complexType>
    <xsd:attribute name="name"    type="xsd:string"/>
    <xsd:attribute name="owner"   type="xsd:string"/>
    <xsd:attribute name="address" type="xsd:string"/>
  </xsd:complexType>
</xsd:element>
```

SEE ALSO <!ELEMENT>, Elements

Schema Entities

The best way to declare an entity in an XML Schema is to declare the entity as an element with a fixed value. For instance, assume you are replacing the copyright symbol (©), shown in the following example using a DTD, with a Schema statement:

```
<?xml version="1.0" ?>
<!DOCTYPE copyright [
<!ENTITY copy "#169">
]>
<copyright xmlns="http://www.mysite.com/copyright" >
 <!-- etc -->
  <statement>Copyright &copy; 2002. All rights
  reserved.</statement>
 <!-- etc -->
</copyright>
```

in order to replace this DTD entity declaration with a Schema statement, such as

```
<xsd:element name="copy" type="xsd:token"
fixed="&#169"/>
```

This element can be used in an XML document using the following code:

```
<?xml version="1.0" ?>
<copyright xmlns="http://www.mysite.com/copyright">
 <!-- etc -->
  <statement>Copyright <copy/> </statement>
 <!-- etc -->
</copyright>
```

SEE ALSO *Data Types, Entities*

Schema Groups

Groups aid in the sorting of elements and attributes into easily interpreted categories, or they can be used as a means of providing a shorthand notation for selections of elements applied to multiple <complexTypes>.

Element Groups

Use the <group> element, shown in the following example, to create group-ings out of elements used in multiple places in your XML Schema:

```xml
<xsd:group name="CustomerInfo">

 <xsd:sequence>

   <xsd:element name="customer">

      <xsd:complexType>

      <xsd:element name="name" type="xsd:string"/>

       <xsd:element name="address"
       type="xsd:string"/>

      <xsd:element name="city" type="xsd:string" />

      <xsd:element name="state" type="xsd:string" />

      <xsd:element name="zip" type="xsd:decimal" />

      </xsd:complexType>

   </xsd:element>

 </xsd:sequence>

</xsd:group>
```

Groups do not define datatypes, they define containers holding sets of el-ements or/and attributes to be used to describe complex types.

Attribute Groups

Attribute groups work like parameter entities in DTDs, allowing you to avoid redefining attributes used by multiple elements in your document.

The following example creates a group of attributes that are used in both the InvoiceLineItem and OrderLineItem element declarations.

NOTE   *Both the individual attribute declarations and attribute group references must appear at the end of complex type definitions.*

```xml
<!-- Attribute group declaration -->

<xsd:attributeGroup name="itemdescription">

 <xsd:attribute name="itemnum" type="xsd:short"/>
```

```
   <xsd:attribute name="itemname"  type="xsd:decimal"/>
    <xsd:attribute name="supplier">
      <xsd:simpleType>
       <xsd:restriction base="xsd:string">
         <xsd:enumeration value="Toll House"/>
         <xsd:enumeration value="Toastmaster"/>
         <xsd:enumeration value="Keebler"/>
        </xsd:restriction>
       </xsd:simpleType>
     </xsd:attribute>
     <xsd:attribute name="quantity" type="xsd:boolean"/>
     <xsd:attribute name="cost"  type="xsd:decimal"/>
  </xsd:attributeGroup>


<!-- Element declarations using the previously
      declared attribute group -->
<xsd:element name="invoicelineitem"
               minOccurs="0" maxOccurs="unbounded">
  <xsd:complexType>
   <xsd:sequence>
    <xsd:element name="itemname" type="xsd:string"/>
    <xsd:element name="itemdescription"
    type="xsd:string" />
   </xsd:sequence>
   <!-- attributeGroup replaces individual
   declarations -->
   <xsd:attributeGroup ref="itemdescription"/>
  </xsd:complexType>
</xsd:element>
```

```
<xsd:element name="orderlineitem"
           minOccurs="0" maxOccurs="unbounded">
<xsd:complexType>
  <xsd:attributeGroup ref="itemdescription"/>
  <xsd:attribute name="numonhand"
             type="xsd:nonnegativeinteger"/>
</xsd:complexType>
</xsd:element>
```

Attribute groups improve the readability of Schemas, making it easier to update the Schema with all of the attributes being defined and edited in one location.

NOTE   *Attribute groups may contain other attribute groups.*

SEE ALSO *Entities, Schemas*

Schema Regular Expressions

Regular expressions used in Schemas are very similar to regular expressions used in other programming and development languages. The following table shows the use of regular expressions in schemas:

EXPRESSION	MATCH(S)	DESCRIPTION
[0-9]x	1x 5x 0x 9x	Numerical character followed by the character x.
ab{2}x	abbx	The characters 'a' and two 'b' preceding 'x.'
ab{2,4}x	abbx, abbbx, abbbbx	The characters 'a' and between two and four 'b' preceding 'x.'
(ab){2}x	ababx	The character combination 'ab' occurring twice before 'x.'
(a|b)+x	ax, bx, aax, abx, bax, bbx,	Any combination of 'a' and/or 'b' preceding 'x.'

EXPRESSION	MATCH(S)	DESCRIPTION
.*abc.*	1x2abc, abc1x2, z3456abchooray	Any number of characters preceding or following the string 'abc.'
[abcde]x	ax, bx, cx, dx, ex	Any one of the letters 'a,' 'b,' 'c,' 'd,' or 'e' preceding 'x.'
[a-e]x	ax, bx, cx, dx, ex	Any one of the letters 'a,' 'b,' 'c,' 'd,' or 'e' preceding 'x.'
[-ae]x	-x, ax, ex	Any of the characters 'a,' 'e,' or '-' preceding 'x.'
[a-e-[bd]]x	ax, cx, ex	Any of the characters 'a' through 'e,' other than 'b' or 'd' preceding 'x.'
a*x	x, ax, aax, aaax	Zero or more 'a' characters preceding 'x.'
a?x	ax, x	Zero or one 'a' character preceding 'x.'
a+x	ax, aax, aaax	One or more 'a' characters preceding 'x.'
\d	1, 2, 3	A single digit.
\Dx	2x @x	Nondigit character fol lowed by the character x.
\p{IsGreek}	Ö×ØÙ	Greek characters. The Is construction may be applied to any block name (for example, "Greek") as defined by UNICODE.
\P{IsGreek}	A b 2 C &	Non-Greek characters. The Is construction may be applied to any block name (for example, "Greek") as defined by UNICODE.

EXPRESSION	MATCH(S)	DESCRIPTION
\p{Lu}	A B C	Uppercase characters. The value of \p{} (for example, "Lu") is defined by UNICODE.
string\s\d	string 1, string 5	A string followed by a white-space character (space, tab, new line) and a single digit.
string\s\w	string word	A string followed by a single white-space character and a word.
.x	8x cx ^x	Any character followed by the character x.

These regular expressions would be used when defining your own simple type. For instance, the following example defines an e-mail type:

```
<xsd:simpleType name="email">

    <xsd:restriction base="xsd:string">

        <xsd:pattern value=.*@.*/>

    </xsd:restriction>

</xsd:simpleType>
```

SEE ALSO *Boolean Logic, Schema Data Types*

Schema Syntax

Writing a basic Schema is essentially the same as creating a XML document. The structure and punctuation is the same, but you are describing the XML elements found within your document. The following XML document describes a series of purchase orders as the foundation document for our Schema example:

```
<purchaseorders lastupdated="21-09-03">

<order orderid="03-9876">

  <customer custid="CYP0986">

    <name> R. Cypher </name>
```

155

```
    <address> Osborne, WY </address>
  </customer>
  <items>
    <lineitem>
      <itemname> Scissors </itemname>
      <itemcost> 5.99 </itemcost>
    </lineitem>
    <lineitem>
      <itemname> Paper </itemname>
      <itemcost> 1.99 </itemcost>
    </lineitem>
    <lineitem>
      <itemname> Legal Pads 10pk </itemname>
      <itemcost> 11.99 </itemcost>
    </lineitem>
  </items>
</order>
<order ordered="03-9877">
  <customer custid="COC8721">
    <name> B. Cocker </name>
    <address> Tempest, WY </address>
  </customer>
  <items>
    <lineitem>
      <itemname> Zebra Pens 10pk</itemname>
      <itemcost> 19.99 </itemcost>
    </lineitem>
    <lineitem>
      <itemname> Xerox Paper </itemname>
```

```
<itemcost> 17.99 </itemcost>

    </lineitem>

  </items>

</order>

</purchaseorders>
```

You can create a Schema based upon this document using either a hierarchical or flat catalog layout. No matter which style is used to define your Schema, you must open with an xsd:schema element following the <?xml?> declaration.

```
<?xml version="1.0" encoding="utf-8"?>

<xsd:schema xmlns:xsd="http://www.w3.org/2000/10/
XMLSchema">
```

A Hierarchical Schema

A hierarchical Schema is written in the same order as the document itself. To match the start tag for the <purchaseorder> element, we define an element named "purchaseorder." This element has attributes and nontext children and is therefore considered a <complexType> (since the other datatype, <simpleType>, is reserved for datatypes holding only values and no elements or attributes).

```
<xsd:element name="purchaseorder">

  <xsd:complexType>

<!— Insert other Element Definitions. —>

  </xsd:complexType>

</xsd:element>
```

With the <purchaseorder> element defined as an element of a complex type, you need to define the remainder of its child elements. In the following code, the <order> element is defined as another complex element because it contains its own set of child elements. Since this element can occur many times or not at all, you must use the minOccurs and the maxOccurs Schema attributes to identify an acceptable number of <order> child elements of the <purchaseorder> element.

```
<xsd:element name="order"

    minOccurs="0" maxOccurs="unbounded">

  <xsd:complexType>
```

157

```
<!-- Insert other Element Definitions. -->
</xsd:complexType>
</xsd:element>
```

The <sequence> element contains the list of child elements of the order element, which are both complex types: <customer> and<items>.

```
<xsd:sequence>
  <xsd:element name="customer">
    <xsd:complexType>
    <!-- Insert other Element Definitions. -->
    </xsd:complexType>
  </xsd:element>
  <xsd:element name="items">
    <xsd:complexType>
    <!-- Insert other Element Definitions. -->
    </xsd:complexType>
  </xsd:element>
</xsd:sequence>
```

NOTE   *The xsd: namespace prefix identifies the origin of schema elements, when the Schema is included within the XML document.*

Now define the two elements that are children of the <customer> element: <name> and <address>. These are simple string elements without any child elements of their own, or applied attributes.

```
<xsd:element name="name" type="xsd:string"/>
<xsd:element name="address" type="xsd:string"/>
```

NOTE   *The type (xsd:string) is prefixed by the schema namespace, indicating a predefined XML Schema datatype. This process goes beyond the implications made in the XML Namespaces recommendation.*

You then add in the <lineitem> element as another complex datatype, and child of the <items> element. Since this element can occur many times or not at all, you must use the minOccurs and the maxOccurs Schema attributes to identify an acceptable number of <lineitem> child elements of the <items>

element. At this point, you can also specify the list of all the <lineitem> element's child elements in the same manner as the <name> and <address> elements.

```
<xsd:element name="lineitem"
      minOccurs="0" maxOccurs="unbounded">
  <xsd:complexType>
    <xsd:sequence>
     <xsd:element name="itemname" type="xsd:string"/>
     <xsd:element name="itemcost" type="xsd:string"/>
    </xsd:sequence>
  </xsd:complexType>
</xsd:element>
```

At this point, all of the elements in the document have been defined, and our schema looks like the following:

```
<?xml version="1.0" encoding="utf-8"?>
<xsd:schema xmlns:xsd="http://www.w3.org/2000/10/
XMLSchema">
<xsd:element name="purchaseorder">
  <xsd:complexType>
    <xsd:element name="order"
          minOccurs="0" maxOccurs="unbounded">
      <xsd:complexType>
        <xsd:sequence>
          <xsd:element name="customer">
            <xsd:complexType>
              <xsd:element name="name"
              type="xsd:string"/>
               <xsd:element name="address"
              type="xsd:string"/>
            </xsd:complexType>
          </xsd:element>
```

```
<xsd:element name="items">

  <xsd:complexType>

    <xsd:element name="lineitem"

         minOccurs="0"
         maxOccurs="unbounded">

      <xsd:complexType>

        <xsd:sequence>

          <xsd:element name="itemname"
          type="xsd:string"/>

          <xsd:element name="itemcost"
          type="xsd:string"/>

        </xsd:sequence>

      </xsd:complexType>

    </xsd:element>

    </xsd:complexType>

  </xsd:element>

  </xsd:sequence>

  </xsd:complexType>

</xsd:element>

</xsd:complexType>

</xsd:element>
```

Keep in mind that none of the attributes of the <purchaseorder>, <order>, and <customer> elements have been added to this schema.

The following statement declares the attribute of the <purchaseorder> element:

```
<xsd:attribute name="lastupdated"
type="xsd:date"/>
```

This statement is inserted following the closing <xsd:sequence> element of the <purchaseorder> but before its closing <xsd:complexType> element.

The attribute definition for the <order> element's orderid attribute is

```
<xsd:attribute name="orderid" type="xsd:string"/>
```

The attribute definition for the <customer> element's custid attribute is

```
<xsd:attribute name="custid" type="xsd:string"/>
```

Once added to the Schema, it will appear as shown in the following example. The added attributes are shown in boldfaced text.

```
<?xml version="1.0" encoding="utf-8"?>

<xsd:schema xmlns:xsd="http://www.w3.org/2000/10/
XMLSchema">

<xsd:element name="purchaseorder">

  <xsd:complexType>

    <xsd:element name="order"

        minOccurs="0" maxOccurs="unbounded

      <xsd:complexType>

        <xsd:sequence>

          <xsd:element name="customer">

            <xsd:complexType>

              <xsd:element name="name"
              type="xsd:string"/>

              <xsd:element name="address"
              type="xsd:string"/>

              <xsd:attribute name="custid"
              type="xsd:string"/>

            </xsd:complexType>

          </xsd:element>

          <xsd:element name="items">

            <xsd:complexType>

              <xsd:element name="lineitem"

                  minOccurs="0"
                  maxOccurs="unbounded">

                <xsd:complexType>

                  <xsd:sequence>

                    <xsd:element name="itemname"
                    type="xsd:string"/>
```

```
        <xsd:element name="itemcost"
        type="xsd:string"/>

      </xsd:sequence>

    </xsd:complexType>

  </xsd:element>

</xsd:complexType>

</xsd:element>

</xsd:sequence>

<xsd:attribute name="orderid"
 type="xsd:string"/>

</xsd:complexType>

</xsd:element>

<xsd:attribute name="lastupdated"
 type="xsd:date"/>

</xsd:complexType>

</xsd:element>
```

NOTE   *Attribute definitions must always follow the element definitions. This rule is imposed by the World Wide Web Consortium Schema Working Group, which specified an order to the definitions of listed element and attributes within a <complexType> element.*

Flat Catalog of Schema Elements

By organizing your element definitions into groups, you make them easier for people to read without affecting the software using your Schema. By grouping element definitions, you avoid having deeply embedded elements, created using a hierarchical Schema structure.

A flat catalog describes each element, child element, and attribute in easily understood groupings. References point to where child elements and attributes are defined for <complexType> elements using this structure.

```
<?xml version="1.0" encoding="utf-8"?>

<xsd:schema xmlns:xsd="http://www.w3.org/2000/10/
XMLSchema">

<!-- definition of simple type elements -->

  <xsd:element name="name" type="xsd:string"/>
```

```xml
      <xsd:element name="address" type="xsd:string"/>
      <xsd:element name="itemname" type="xsd:string"/>
      <xsd:element name="itemcost" type="xsd:string"/>


  <!-- definition of attributes -->
      <xsd:attribute name="lastupdated"
      type="xsd:date"/>
      <xsd:attribute name="orderid" type="xsd:string"/>
      <xsd:attribute name="custid" type="xsd:string"/>


  <!-- definition of complex type elements -->
    <xsd:element name="lineitem">
    <xsd:complexType>
      <xsd:sequence>
        <!-- simple type elements are referenced using
        "ref" attribute  -->
        <xsd:element ref="itemname"/>
        <xsd:element ref="itemcost"/>
      </xsd:sequence>
    </xsd:complexType>
    </xsd:element>


    <xsd:element name="items">
     <xsd:complexType>
       <xsd:element ref="lineitem"
            minOccurs="0" maxOccurs="unbounded"/>
     </xsd:complexType>
    </xsd:element>


    <xsd:element name="customer">
```

```
       <xsd:complexType>

         <xsd:sequence>

           <!-- simple type elements are referenced using
           "ref" attribute  -->

           <xsd:element ref="name"/>

           <xsd:element ref="address"/>

         </xsd:sequence>

         <xsd:attribute ref="custid"/>

       </xsd:complexType>

     </xsd:element>


     <xsd:element name="order">

       <xsd:complexType>

         <xsd:sequence>

           <xsd:element ref="customer"/>

           <xsd:element ref="items"/>

         </xsd:sequence>

         <xsd:attribute ref="orderid"/>

       </xsd:complexType>

     </xsd:element>


     <xsd:element name="purchasorders">

       <xsd:complexType>

         <xsd:element ref="order"

             minOccurs="0" maxOccurs="unbounded"/>

         <xsd:attribute ref="lastupdated"/>

       </xsd:complexType>

     </xsd:element>


   </xsd:schema>
```

By using the ref attribute to reference a previously created element or attribute, you essentially clone the previously defined element or attribute. You are not redefining the object, because the name and type are specified only once. This method allows you to reference it multiple times, to apply them to complexType elements as needed.

Schema Validators and Parsers

Schema validators and parsers check XML and Schema documents for well-formed structure and validity. This software runs either on your local machine, as does MSXML 4.0b2, or on a network, such as the Internet, as does the World Wide Web Consortium's Validator.

W3C Validator for XML Schema

The World Wide Web Consortium (W3C) provides an online Schema validator at *http://www.w3.org/2000/09/webdata/xsv*. Although still undergoing testing, it allows you to test any document or Schema accessible through the Internet. Provide the address of the document, as shown in Figure S-3, to receive a report listing all the warnings, errors, and problems encountered during validation.

Figure S-3   W3C Validator for XML Schemas.

Microsoft XML Parser 4.0b2

The Microsoft XML Parser, shown in Figure S4, processes Schemas and DTDs. It is available for download from *http://msdn.microsoft.com/xml/* and runs with Internet Explorer 5. The MSXML Parser includes these features:

- XSD validation with SAX
- XSD validation with the DOM
- Faster processing and parsing of documents

SEE ALSO *DTD, Parsers, XML Software*

Scripting

Scripting is the process of adding JavaScript or VBScript programs to your XML documents. These scripts can perform a myriad of tasks including the formatting, and automatic testing of information contained within the document, the update of that information as the document viewers interact with the information.

SEE ALSO *ECMAScript, Java, JavaScript, Jscript, VBScript*

Scriptlets see JavaScript

Servers

The computers that "serve-up" documents stored for distribution are called servers. There are all kinds of servers that work with Web documents, including FTP servers, database servers, and HTTP servers. XML documents are typically distributed through the use of database or HTTP servers, although they can be created on the fly by e-commerce programs and other utilities.

SEE ALSO *Database, E-Commerce, HTTP, Servers*

SGML

XML has its foundation in the Standard Generalized Markup Language (SGML). This language was developed as a means of identifying the portions and content of a document not by the actual content or line numbers, but by the type of information that it contained. For example, you could use SGML marked up documents and search for a string such as heading1 to identify a level-one heading, no matter what the content of that heading might be. You could then use scripts to find all of the level-one headings by looking for that heading1 text marker. You can use scripts to show only the level-one headings or copy them into another document to create a table of contents. You could also use scripts to sort out the text that isn't a level-one heading.

SGML was developed out of the General Markup Language (GML), an undertaking by a few of IBM's employees in the late 1960s. Very few organizations, educational institutions, and government offices used this language until it became a standard in 1986. Shortly before its official adoption as a standard, the Internal Revenue Service and the Department of Defense began using SGML and requiring their contractors to use it also. Then with the explosion of the Internet, SGML became the "parent" of XML and HTML.

HTML, unlike SGML and XML, controls the presentation of information. SGML and XML identify document content so that information can be formatted consistently throughout the document. Both SGML and XML are best suited for use in documents that have large amounts of similarly organized information, such as catalogs, address books, mathematical functions, and even accounting records.

SEE ALSO *HTML, Markup Languages, XML*

SQL

The Standard Query Language (SQL) is the primary language used to collect information normally stored on database systems. SQL uses a series of SELECT statements to sort through information that is stored in a collection of tables and then display that information in a format that can be used in a meaningful fashion. SQL statements are commonly used to collect information from databases and display it as documents to Web site visitors as catalogs, purchase orders, or even test results.

SEE ALSO *Database*

Standarization

Standardization is the process by which standards are created which provide structure for the language, syntax, and semantics to be used in the creation of technology. The World Wide Web Consortium (W3C) is one of the largest standards organizations for document formats associated with the Internet. The XML standard went through the standardization process, and each of its child languages continues to go through that evaluation process.

As XML, and the internet, continue to grow there will constantly be languages undergoing the standardization process.

SEE ALSO *HTML, SGML, XHTML, XML, XML Applications*

Start-Tag

The start-tag of an XML element is the opening tag. All elements have a start-tag. Start-tags contain all of the attributes that are used with the element, for example:

```
<elementname>
```

SEE ALSO *<!ELEMENT>, Elements, End-Tag*

Structuring Data

One of the most important parts of creating an XML document is the sorting of information into elements and attributes. Your choice of which items to put into elements, and which to format into attributes, will be somewhat dependant upon which type of style sheet you are planning on using. If you wish to use Cascading Style Sheets, then keep in mind that it can't display the contents of attributes, so all of the information you wish to be displayed will have to be in an element. XSL can display the contents of attributes, so your choice won't be subject to that stipulation.

Elements

Elements are typically made from large pieces of information. Information such as names, descriptions, and prices are typically stored in elements. These are the same types of information that would be stored in a field in a database.

Attributes

Attributes are typically made from descriptive items of information. For example, the item number of an item makes a good attribute, if your forms display only the item name and description. Titles, such as Mr., Mrs., or Dr., are also often used as attributes. Identification numbers that keep track of records apart from the content of the records themselves tend to be used as attributes.

SEE ALSO *Attributes, Elements*

Style Rule

Style rules control the formatting of information in your XML document. The formatting of the individual rules will be dependent upon the style sheet type that you choose to use. Within the style sheet, you will need to specify how every element is treated, unless you wish it to be treated in the same fashion as its parent.

SEE ALSO *Cascading Style Sheets, Hierarchies, Inheritance, Style Sheets, Tree Structures, XSL*

Style Sheets

Style sheets are documents allowing you to globally alter the appearance of every item found within your XML document, or a series of XML documents, without changing the document markup. Style sheets allow you to control the size of fonts, font colors, document or object backgrounds, object borders, and speech synthesizer controls, as well as multiple visual and audio effects for XML information. XML documents typically use either Cascading Style Sheets (CSS) or the Extensible Stylesheet Language (XSL), although the Document Style Semantics and Specification Language (DSSSL) is also available.

Cascading Style Sheets

Cascading Style Sheets (CSS) format the appearance of document information using properties that are interpreted by document browsers and other applications. CSS works by setting property values controlling object appearance, and implementing cascade rules for controlling which property values are used, and which are superseded by the document browser and/or other Cascading Style Sheets. Cascading Style Sheets are supported by all of the major Web browsers, in some form or another, including Netscape Navigator 4.5–6.x, Opera 4.x and 5, and Microsoft's Internet Explorer 4.x–5.x.

NOTE *Support for Cascading Style Sheets in Netscape Navigator 4.x was quite limited and should not be considered a viable testing platform for CSS.*

Extensible Stylesheet Language

The Extensible Stylesheet Language (XSL) provides for more flexibility of functions than Cascading Style Sheets (CSS), although it does not have the same amount of software support. XSL is currently supported only by Netscape Navigator 6 (*http://www.netscape.com*) and Internet Explorer 5.5 (*http://www.microsoft.com*) after upgrading Internet Explorer's MSXML parser (*http://msdn.microsoft.com/xml*). Be aware that neither of these products supports XSL fully.

XSL contains two parts, the Extensible Stylesheet Language Transformations (XSLT) and the XSL Formatting properties. XSLT converts XML document information into another format, such as HTML, so that it can be easily read by other applications. The XSL Formatting properties work similar to CSS, by formatting the information contained within your XML document during an XSL transformation.

DSSSL

The Document Style Semantics and Specification Language (DSSSL) is a standard typically used in processing SGML documents, although it can be used with XML. DSSSL describes how the structure of SGML documents are visually presented, converted, and processed by supporting applications. SGML is a document structure language. DSSSL is a document processing language more similar to XSLT than CSS. DSSSL can convert XML documents into another form. For instance, DSSSL could convert an XML document into an HTML document, a format that could easily be imported into a database, or even a PDF file.

SEE ALSO *Cascading Style Sheets, XSL, XSL-FO, XSLT*

Syntax

Document syntax is the formal way that all parts of a language are formatted and structured. This structure controls the interpretation of the language so that all of its individual parts are properly handled and manipulated within the confines of the application. In the case of an XML document, this is proper syntax:

```
<order order_id="99-098"> </order>
```

On the other hand, this statement is invalid XML, but proper CSS:

```
order  { font: Arial red ; }
```

This statement would be invalid in either language:

```
[order font is red]
```

SEE ALSO *<!ATTLIST>, <!ELEMENT>, Cascading Style Sheets, HTML, Schemas, XML, XSL*

Tags

The terms *element* and *tag* are often used interchangeably, but they are not necessarily the same thing. A tag is the complete syntax, including punctuation, which surrounds the name of the element. The element is the name with its implied function. For example, order is the name of an element, while <order> is a tag.

SEE ALSO *Elements*

Templates

Documents made to be reused are often referred to as templates. You can create XML templates by creating an empty structure as shown below, and then simply filling in the information as necessary:

```
<purchaseorders lastupdated="">
<order orderid="">
  <customer custid=" ">
    <name> </name>
    <address> </address>
  </customer>
  <items>
    <lineitem>
      <itemname> </itemname>
      <itemcost> </itemcost>
    </lineitem>
  </items>
</order>
<order ordered=" ">
  <customer custid=" ">
    <name> </name>
    <address> </address>
  </customer>
  <items>
```

171

```
<lineitem>

    <itemname> </itemname>

    <itemcost> </itemcost>

  </lineitem>

 </items>

</order>

</purchaseorders>
```

In the world of XML, DTDs and Schemas also provide a template for the creation of XML documents. XML editors, such as XML Spy, allow you to create XML documents based upon the document structure identified within that DTD or Schema. This makes the creation of multiple documents based on a single validation source possible, without the potential inclusion of document structure errors, which would occur if you were attempting to rewrite the XML structure by hand.

SEE ALSO *DTD, Entities, Schemas*

Tree Structures

XML documents use an inverted tree structure with elements used as a set of nodes for the branching of information contained within the document. You can trace the structure of your XML document through the same type of system that you use when tracking a family genealogy.

SEE ALSO *Ancestor, Node, Parent Elements, Root Elements*

Troubleshooting

Although XML documents are just text files, they are processed by parsers and validators to ensure that the structure of the document is well-formed and readable by any XML application aware of the meaning of your elements. Because these files are processed, a variety of errors can occur during that time. Even something as simple as a period in the wrong spot can break an XML document, a DTD, or even a schema.

XML Document Structure Parsing Errors

The error messages shown in the following table can occur when parsing your XML document:

NOTE   *All parsers create a different list of codes, but these should be recognizable in most parsers.*

ERROR MESSAGE	DESCRIPTION
Attribute External Entity Ref	Attribute content contains a reference to an external entity.
Bad Char Ref	An invalid character was found in the element content.
Duplicate Attribute	Two attributes of the same name are used in one element.
Incorrect Encoding	Document format isn't complete.
Invalid Token	Element uses invalid naming scheme.
Misplaced XML PI	The XML processing instruction is in the wrong location.
No Elements	There are no elements in your document.
No Memory	You have run out of memory while parsing the document.
Param Entity Ref	A parameter entity reference was found in the XML document.
Recursive Entity Ref	An entity is referring to itself.
Syntax	Syntax error has been encountered.
Tag Mismatch	Expected to see TagA and found TagB instead.

ERROR MESSAGE	DESCRIPTION
Unclosed CDATA Section	Character Data section is opened, but not closed.
Unclosed Token	Empty element with closing slash missing.
Undefined Entity	A general entity was not defined as a default Entity type.
Unknown Encoding	Document format isn't recognized.

SEE ALSO *Parsers, Validating Documents, XML*

DTD and Schema Parsing Errors

The error messages shown in the following table can occur when parsing your DTD:

NOTE *All parsers create a different list of codes, but these should be recognizable in most parsers.*

ERROR CODE	DESCRIPTION
ATTLIST DUPLICATED ID	Can't define multiple ID attributes on the same element.
ATTLIST ID PRESENCE	An attribute of type ID must have a declared default of #IMPLIED or #REQUIRED.
ATTRIBUTE FIXED	Attribute has a value which does not match the fixed value defined in the DTD/Schema.
ATTRIBUTE NOT DEFINED	An attribute on this element is not defined in the DTD/Schema.

ERROR CODE	DESCRIPTION
ATTRIBUTE VALUE	Attribute has an invalid value according to the DTD/Schema.
DEFAULT ATTRIBUTE	Error in the default attribute value defined in DTD/Schema.
DTD EXPECTING	Missing characters or values in the DTD/Schema.
ELEMENT DEFINED	The element is already declared.
ELEMENT ID NOT FOUND	An attribute references the ID, which is not defined in the document.
ELEMENT NOT COMPLETE	Element content is in complete according to the DTD/Schema.
ELEMENT UNDECLARED	An element is used but not declared in the DTD/Schema.
ELEMENT UNDEFINED	Reference to undeclared element.
EMPTY NOT ALLOWED	Element cannot be empty according to the DTD/Schema.
ENTITY UNDEFINED	Reference to undefined entity in the DTD.
EXTENT IN ATTR	Can't reference an external general parsed entity in an attribute value.
INFINITE ENTITY LOOP	Entity contains an infinite recursive loop.

ERROR CODE	DESCRIPTION
ILLEGAL TEXT	Text is not allowed in this element according to the DTD/Schema.
INVALID CONTENT	Element content is in valid according to the DTD/Schema.
IOERROR	Error opening input file.
LOAD EXTERNALENTITY	Could not load and external entity.
MISSING NOTATION	Declaration contains a reference to undefined notation.
MISSING PE ENTITY	Parameter entity must be defined before it is used.
MIXEDCONTENT DUP NAME	The same name must not appear more than once in a single mixed-content declaration.
MULTI FIXED VALUES	An attribute declaration cannot contain multiple fixed values.
NAME COLON	Entities, PIs, Notations, and NMTOKENS names can't contain a colon.
NAMESPACE URI EMPTY	A namespace, other than the default, has an empty URI.
NDATA INVALID PE	Can't use the NDATA keyword in a parameter entity declaration.
NDATA INVALID REF	Can't use an unparsed entity in an entity reference.

ERROR CODE	DESCRIPTION
NOTATION DEFINED	The notation is already declared.
PARSING ENTITY	Error while parsing entity.
PUBLICID INVALID	The public document ID is invalid.
REQUIRED ATTRIBUTE MISSING	A required attribute is missing.
REQUIRED NDATA	Can't use a general parsed entity as a value for specified attribute.
ROOT NAME MISMATCH	The name of the top-most element doesn't match the name of the DOCTYPE declaration.
STOPPED BY USER	XML parser stopped by user.
UNKNOWN ERROR	Unknown error has occurred.
XMLLANG INVALIDID	The value of the xml:lang attribute is invalid.
XMLNS FIXED	Attribute must be a #FIXED attribute.
XMLNS RESERVED	Reserved namespace cannot be redeclared.
XMLNS UNDEFINED	Reference to undeclared namespace prefix.

XSLT Processing Errors

ERROR CODE	DESCRIPTION
BAD ROOT ELEMENT	The root element of XSLT stylesheet must be <xsl:stylesheet> or <xsl:template>.
INVALID SCRIPT ENGINE	The specified language is not a scripting language.
KEYWORD MAY NOT CONTAIN	The specified keyword may not contain the stated value.
KEYWORD MAY NOT FOLLOW	The specified keyword may not follow the previous statement.
METHOD ERROR	Error returned from a property or method call.
SCRIPT ERROR_LINE	On line = x, col = x from the <xsl:script> tag an error has occurred in the script.
STACK OVERFLOW	The XSLT processor stack has overflowed— probable cause is infinite template recursion.
UNEXPECTED KEYWORD	The specified keyword may not be used here.

SEE **ALSO** *XSL, XSL-FO, XSLT*

Unicode

The Unicode character set is a collection of encoded characters similar to the ISO-10646 standard that identifies all of the printable characters used in the majority of languages in the world. Because each character is encoded at its own code point, the character set is broken down into the world's separate languages, with each taking their own section of the complete character set. Using this one set of characters, the majority of the world's computers can exchange information without ambiguity. Unicode isn't a sorting sequence for characters, nor is it a definition of glyph characters. It is strictly a 16-bit universal character encoding system.

SEE ALSO *Character Set*

URI

A Uniform Resource Identifier (URI) is the combination of the Uniform Resource Name (URN) and the Uniform Resource Locator (URL) that provides a specific point of reference for an item, in a document, anywhere on the Internet.

SEE ALSO *URL, URN, XLink*

URL

A Uniform Resource Locator (URL) is the address of a document on a network such as the Internet. This address, typically in the form of *http://www.myserver.com/adirectory/afile.xml*, is composed of three main parts:

- **http://** Identifies the type of server you are communicating with. In this case it is an HTTP server typically used to distribute documents. Other options for a server designation include ftp://, mailto:, news://, telnet://, and gopher://.

- **www.myserver.com** Identifies the computer or DNS identity of the computer that stores the document you are looking for. This address could also be replaced with the IP address (123.123.123.123) of the computer.

- **/adirectory/afile.xml** Identifies the directory and optional filename of the page to load.

SEE ALSO *URI, URN, XLink*

URN

The Uniform Resource Name (URN) is used to specify the name of an object located within a document. For instance, if you have a document with an object named "cypher_order," you can reference that particular section of the complete order list by using a reference similar to the following:

```
http://www.myserver.com/orders/
purchaseorder.xml#cypher_order
```

SEE ALSO *URI, URL, XLink*

Validating Documents

When using a validating parser, such as the MSXML parser from Microsoft, you are ensuring that your documents are not just well-formed, but that your document's structure itself is documented. You are making sure that your document's structure can be read and used by any number of additional documents and by any number of organizations. The documentation of your XML document is included in either the DTD or the schema document. Since there are very few DTDs or schemas available for public document formats, you will need to write your own from which to validate your documents.

Validating Parsers go through each entry in your XML document and compare it to the DTD or schema provided with the XML code. The DTD or schema is either included as a part of the XML document or as an externally linked file. When the validating parser encounters an error in your code, it displays a message identifying the line of code that contained the error, and the type of error that was encountered.

SEE ALSO *Parsers, Troubleshooting, Well-Formed Documents*

VBScript

VBScript (Visual Basic Script Edition) is a proprietary scripting language developed by Microsoft for use with their Internet Explorer Web browser. VBScript has its foundations in Visual Basic, as the name implies, but it is much simpler in structure and application. Using VBScript, document developers can add interactive controls and manipulate the content of their documents. VBScript is available only with Internet Explorer browsers, and if a document containing VBScript is viewed on Netscape Navigator, the page will load but all of the scripts will be ignored.

SEE ALSO *ECMAScript, JavaScript, JScript, Scripting*

W3C see World Wide Web Consortium

Web Servers see Servers

Well-Formed Documents

Well-formed documents contain only properly formatted and punctuated XML code. They meet all of the following rules:

- The <?xml?> declaration is the first line in the document.

- One root element contains all other elements and that element is properly closed. The root element cannot be recursive.

- All elements are nested properly, for example, <order><item></item></order> rather than <order><item></order></item>.

- All empty elements are closed: image />.

- All character entities are properly encoded: ©.

- All element and attribute names contain only letters, numbers, and the punctuation: period (.), underscore (_), and hyphen (-).

- The first character in all element and attribute names is either a letter or the underscore (_) character.

- Comments appear properly bracketed (<!-- -->) and are not nested.

- Comments do not appear inside of elements.

- No attribute names are repeated in a start-tag.

- All attributes are specified in the start-tag of the elements.

- Attribute values don't contain the greater-than (>) character.

SEE ALSO *Parsers, Validating Documents*

White Space

White space in an XML document is any space, tab, or blank line that is inserted into the document to make the markup text contained in the document easier for people to read. This white space isn't typically intended to be passed on to the XML application, and it is therefore ignored in any amount greater than a single-space character. The xml:space attribute controls how white space is treated, allowing you to force the document to preserve white space when necessary.

SEE ALSO *xml:space*

World Wide Web Consortium

Tim Berners-Lee created the World Wide Web Consortium (W3C) in 1994 while at the Massachusetts Institute of Technology, Laboratory for Computer Science (MIT/LCS). This process was undertaken with CERN and received support from DARPA and the European Commission. The W3C develops specifications, guidelines, software, and tools to lead the Web to its full potential. The Web is now the primary medium for the transfer of information, commerce, and communication between individuals, business, educational institutes, and governments around the world.

At this point, the W3C has more than 500 member organizations from around the globe that work together to promote interoperability and encourage an open forum for discussion. In the last five years, the W3C has developed 35+ technical specifications describing the Web's internal structure. These specifications will help make the Web a robust source of information for individuals around the world. The W3C's goals for the Web are as follows:

- Make the Web accessible to all through the promotion of technologies that work on all continents, and take into account the material and resource limitations of those areas.

- Develop an environment permitting everyone to make the best use of Web resources.

- Guide the Web's development with consideration toward the commercial and social issues raised by the use of this technology.

SEE ALSO *CERN, ECMA, ISO*

XHTML

The Extensible Hypertext Markup Language (XHTML) is a reformulation of the HTML 4.0 specification into modules that follow the rules imposed by XML. XHTML uses the existing language of the HTML 4.1 specification and continues to support the HTML DOM. XHTML allows document authors to create documents that will be functional in the future XML-centric world and still work in today's HTML-centric Web.

NOTE   *The XHTML specification is located on the W3C Web site at* http:/ /www.w3.org/MarkUp/.

SEE ALSO *HTML, Markup Languages, XML*

XLink

The XML Linking Language (XLink) creates and defines links between resources in XML documents. This specification creates more informative and flexible links than available in the linking abilities of HTML documents. XLink provides a framework for creating a wide variety of links from a basic unidirectional link to more complex linking structures allowing XML documents to do the following:

- Create links between more than two resources.

- Associate metadata with the link.

- Create databases of links capable of being located away from the linked documents and resources.

NOTE   *The World Wide Web Consortium stores their information on the XML Linking Language at* http://www.w3.org/TR/2001/REC-xlink-20010627/.

The basic structure of an XLink is

```
<mylinks:xref

  xmlns:mylinks="http://myserver.com/"

  xmlns:xlink="http://www.w3.org/1999/xlink"

  xlink:type="simple"

  xlink:href="orders.xml"

  xlink:role="http://www.myserver.com/orderslist"

  xlink:title="Purchase Orders List"

  xlink:show="new"

  xlink:actuate="onRequest">

 Current List of Purchase Orders

 </mylinks:xref>
```

SEE ALSO *XML Base, XPath, XPointer*

XML

The Extensible Markup Language (XML) is a set of rules specifying how to define markup tags identifying document parts and sub-parts. XML is a markup language similar in structure to HTML, but defined so that it can be used in any industry. XML is the epitome of extensibility for document structures. XML can be personalized for every corporate or private endeavor to which it's applied. XML is easy to read for computers (and not too difficult for humans), easy to debug, and easy to use to create markup languages suitable for any industry using structured data, such as spreadsheets, databases, financial information, and technical drawings.

The beauty of XML is that it allows multiple teams of designers to use the same document structures in multiple documents, and then have these documents viewable by anyone in the organization. This alleviates the need for conversion of documents between departments or businesses that share information.

XML Syntax

XML's tags describe the structure of a document, as well as identifying the content of a document. XML document syntax has the following rules:

- XML tags are opened and closed with angle brackets (< and >) which enclose the identifying name, or label, for the content.

- The content being marked up by the XML elements appears between a start-tag and an end-tag: <element> content </element>.

- All elements must have an end-tag using the exact name (XML is case specific) as the start-tag, other than the addition of a forward slash to the opening angle bracket: </elementname>.

- XML elements can include attributes that provide additional information about the content of the tag or the tag itself. Attributes are matched sets of name/value pairs in the form of name="value". These attributes reside within the tags themselves, as shown in the following code snippet:

```
<element attributename="attributevalue"> content
</element>
```

- All attribute values must be enclosed in quotation marks.

- All elements must be nested properly: <order><customer></customer></order> not <order><customer></order></customer>.

XML parsers can't ignore errors and are required to display errors that occur during the parsing of the document. This makes debugging XML documents easy because you are given a list of errors, including lines numbers and error descriptions. Rules controlling how the document must be marked up affect the well-formedness of the document. A document is well formed if it meets the stated criteria identified within the XML specification. A well-formed document will create no parsing errors.

XML Document Tree

XML documents follow a logical flow and progression that creates an inverted document tree. The primary element in an XML document is called the root. This is the element that serves as a parent or ancestor for the other elements contained within the document. Elements directly beneath the root are children of the root element. Any element defined within another element is that element's child. Any element that is structurally above another is a parent element. All elements in a document are the descendants of the document root. These elements are all contained within the global scope of the document.

The structure that XML gives to its document content becomes an inverted tree, if you were to break each set of markup tags into its own branch on a document. This tree structure allows you to easily see the architecture and tag hierarchy of the XML application.

XML Document Goals

The specification, which identified the goals for XML, was released in February 1998. This standard identifies the requirements of a well-formed XML document, as well as the origin and goals of XML. The goals of XML include the following ideals:

- XML shall easily be implemented over the Internet.
- XML shall be usable across multiple industries and applications.
- XML shall be compatible with SGML.
- XML documents shall be readable by people.
- XML documents shall be capable of being designed swiftly.
- XML document design shall be formal and to the point.
- XML documents must be easy to create.
- XML markup does not need to be terse.

XML and DTDs

Document Type Definitions (DTDs) provide the rules for validating XML documents. DTDs provide instructions, using Backus-Naur Form (BNF) grammar, for identifying which elements are valid for a particular document, and which attributes are valid to use with each element. DTDs list all of the elements, attributes, notations, and entities available for use within a single XML document. DTDs define the relationship of each part to every other part.

DTDs can be added to your XML document either internally or externally using the <!DOCTYPE> element.

XML and Schemas

XML Schemas, like DTDs, validate documents, but provide more features and controls than DTDs. Schemas define the structure, content, and semantics of XML documents that are shared between many different types of computers and applications. Schemas are be parsed with your XML document during the validation process. Schemas use regular expressions to more tightly constrain the information that elements and attributes can contain.

XML Schemas derive from XML, allowing them to be written using a text editor, or one of the Schema development programs downloadable from the Internet. Schemas require the use of XML Namespaces to separate the Schema definition from the XML elements allowing the Schema and markup to exist in a single file.

XML and the DOM

The Document Object Model (DOM) is an application programming interface (API) that describes document structure, and how to access that structure. This means that the DOM provides a platform and language independent method for allowing programs and scripts to access and update the content, structure, and style sheets associated with an XML document. An API provides the standard model for how XML content and elements can be manipulated using scripts. Using the DOM, scripts can be used to give XML pages the ability to show content based upon visitor interactions.

A Basic XML Example

The easiest way to create an XML document is to use a text editor, such as Windows Notepad, Macintosh BBEdit, or Linux emacs, and simply type.

```
<?xml version="1.0" standalone="yes"?>

<introduction>

   Hello Everyone. My name is Fred!

</introduction>
```

Save XML documents with the .xml extension, for example, introduction.xml.

SEE ALSO <!DOCTYPE>, Attributes, Declarations, DTD, ECMAScript, Elements, Hierarchies, JavaScript, JScript, Parsers, Nodes, Parent Elements, Processing Instructions, Schemas, Tree Structure, Validating Documents, VBScript, Well-Formed Documents, XML Applications

xml:Lang

The XML attribute, xml:lang, identifies the language used to display the contents of the specified element. If you are familiar with HTML, this attribute performs the same function as the lang attribute. A set of predefined codes identifies the language being used to create the content of the element to which the attribute is applied. This attribute is especially useful when attempting to display text in a variety of languages. For example, both of the following statements say the same thing. The first is designated as English (en) by the xml:lang attribute; the second as Spanish (sp):

```
<little_ditty xml:lang="en">

Hello! Partner.

</little_ditty >

<little_ditty xml:lang="sp">

Hola! Amigo.

</little_ditty >
```

XML processors display only the document elements corresponding to their language setup. In other words, my computer would display the English statement, but my friend's computer would show the Spanish version. This allows your XML application to automatically adjust a document to your software's capabilities. An alternative is to use external entities to hold copies of the document in each language. This would then allow you to show only that one language that is appropriate when the document is needed.

SEE ALSO Attributes, Entities

xml:space

xml:space controls white space usage within elements. Unlike HTML, where white space is typically unimportant, in XML a single additional space could be vitally important. Think about the white space most computer programming languages, such as COBOL, use. In these systems every space controls the interpretation of the given commands and values. Even if you are displaying haiku, the spacing within the text display is important to the legibility of the poem.

XML parsers preserve white space within the contents of elements. Of course, since the majority of our XML document browsers are also HTML browsers, the white space is at that point ignored. With the application of the xml:space attribute, the XML processor is told to keep the white space intact.

xml:space is the only way to force the retention of significant white space within an element. When using a DTD or a schema, you must define the xml:space attribute for all elements in which it is used. The following <!ATTLIST> declaration forces the preservation of spacing in the element's content.

```
<!ATTLIST itemnumber xml:space (default | preserve)
"preserve">
```

NOTE   *Some parsers, including MSXML, will still ignore white space in your elements, even with the xml:space attribute applied. Some of these parsers will have a setting that can be adjusted to force it to respect your document's white space. Read the documentation on your XML parser for information on these settings.*

SEE ALSO *Attributes, White Space*

XML Applications

XML has been used to create a variety of other document languages that are used extensively in educational institutions, businesses, and on the Internet. Some of these languages are introduced here.

BizTalk

BizTalk is an XML-based document framework that facilitates the exchange of information between businesses and business applications. The BizTalk framework facilitates the implementation of XML Schema and a predefined set of XML elements for communication between business applications. You can get more information on BizTalk at *http://www.biztalk.org*.

Channel Definition Format (CDF)

The Channel Definition Format provides the instructions controlling the creation of a Web channel. CDF channels can be collected automatically by subscribers on a predefined schedule. Channels can be created and run off of any Web server. You can read more about CDF from Microsoft's Web site at *http://msdn.microsoft.com/workshop/delivery/cdf/reference/CDF.asp* or the W3C's site located at *http://www.w3.org/TR/NOTE-CDFsubmit.html*.

Chemical Markup Language (CML)

The Chemical Markup Language (CML) is a set of predefined XML elements that provide for the markup of complex chemical data. CML was created to solve the problem of sharing chemical information across the Internet in a way that was modifiable. Previous to the CML language, chemists had to create images that displayed the appropriate chemical equations. You can read more about CML from *http://www.xml-cml.org*.

HTML+Time

Microsoft's HTML + Time draft combines a selection of timing elements with HTML to add a third dimension to Web pages. Using HTML + Time you can control the appearance of images, layers, and other elements on your HTML pages. You can read more about HTML+Time at the W3C site at *http://www.w3.org/TR/NOTE-HTMLplusTIME*.

MathML

The Mathematical Markup Language (MathML) provides the structure necessary to create complex mathematical equations, which can be shared over the Internet between any business, educational institution, or individual. Prior to the creation of MathML, math equations, like chemistry equations, had to be shared using graphics or other document formats. You can read more about MathML at the W3C site at *http://www.w3.org/Math/*.

OSD

The Open Software Description format, created by Microsoft, is intended to serve as a means of providing software information, as well as the software itself, to appropriate computers over a network system. Using OSD a company would be able to have employees automatically update their software when they booted their machines through the use of OSD and batch files. This process would save IT personnel the difficulty of manually installing the updated software on everyone's machines individually. Read more about OSD at *http:// www.w3.org/TR/NOTE-OSD.html.*

SMIL

The Synchronized Multimedia Integration Language (SMIL) provides a selection of elements that control the formatting and timing of objects in multimedia presentations. SMIL files can be viewed using RealPlayer and QuickTime. Internet Explorer 5.5 provides some support for SMIL elements. You can read more about SMIL at *http:// www.w3.org/AudioVideo.*

SVG

The Scalable Vector Graphics (SVG) language provides detailed structures for creating vector graphics on Web documents. Because these graphics are created using only text instructions, they are quite small and can downloaded much faster than traditional graphic elements. Read about SVG at the W3C pages at *http://www.w3.org/Graphics/SVG/.*

XHTML

XHTML is the latest version of the HTML language. XHTML contains the same attributes and elements specified in HTML 4, but formatted and modularized to meet the rules of the XML specification. You can read more about XHTML at *http://www.w3.org/MarkUp/.*

SEE ALSO *HTML, XHTML*

XML Base

XLink is the language used in XML documents to define links within the XML code. XML Base emulates the HTML <base> element by providing a reference point for all XLink links. XML Base specifically allows XML document authors to provide a base URI for referencing all relative links found within their documents, including those links to images, other documents and files, style sheets, and DTDs or schemas.

Although XML Base is closely linked to the XLink specification, it is not part of it. It is its own entity, allowing it to be used in conjunction with any other document type, without XLink being present.

The basic structure of an XML Base statement is

```
<order xml:base="http://myserver.com/xmldocs/"

        xmlns:xlink="http://www.w3.org/1999/xlink">
```

SEE ALSO *XLink, XPath, XPointer*

XML Declaration see <?xml?>

XML Dialects see XML Applications

XML Digital Signatures see Digital Signatures

XML Entity see Entities

XML Processor see Parsers

XML Query

The XML Query language provides a mechanism for the XML language to collect information from XML documents just as if they were database resources. Using a system of algebralike statements, you can collect the information you require from a document. For instance, the following statement will collect and list all of the names and addresses of customers in the orders document:

```
for c in order0/customer do

customer [ c/name, c/address ]
```

You can create queries to check for all records, a single record, or a record based upon an attribute's presence or an attribute's value. You can even sort your results so that directly from the query your collected information is in the order that you wish it to appear.

XML Queries are still undergoing development at the World Wide Web Consortium (W3C) and are not yet implemented in any of the popular browsers.

NOTE   *You can find more information on the XML Query language on the W3C Web site located at* http://www.w3.org/XML/Query.

SEE ALSO *Boolean Logic, SQL, XPath*

XML Software

XML developers use a variety of software to manipulate, create, edit, view, and parse XML documents. The most common, Internet Explorer, uses the MS-XML parser to parse the XML document, which in turns passes the parsed information on to the Web browser. From the user standpoint, you see none of this happening; you simply see the XML contents appear on your screen before you. XML parsers come in a variety of formats, from online resources to ones that you run and store on your personal computer.

SEE ALSO *Parsers*

XPath

The XML Path (XPath) recommendation, completed in November 1999, provides a means of referring to specific portions of an XML document using XSLT and XPointer. This recommendation provides a standard means of referencing addresses and locations within XML documents as well manipulating, and comparing, strings, numbers, and Boolean values.

The following XPath statement would find the <order> tag with the element <ordernumber> set to "99-0876":

```
order[ordernumber="99-0876"]
```

NOTE   *Find out more about XPath at* http://www.w3.org/TR/xpath.

SEE ALSO *XLink, XML Base, XPointer, XSLT*

XPointer

The XML Pointer Language (XPointer) identifies fragments of URI references that locate XML Internet media types, such as text/xml or application/xml. XPointers are used to identify the internal structure of an XML document by selecting specific internal parts of the document based upon information contained in the document tree. Using XPointers, you can select any part of a document, including an element type, an attribute value, character content, and the part's relative position within the document tree.

The following XPointer statement would find an element in your document that has an ID attribute with a value of "AZ987" in the inventorylist.xml document:

```
Inventorylist.xml#xpointer(id("AZ987"))
```

NOTE   *More information is available on XPointer at* http://www.w3.org/
            TR/xptr/.

SEE ALSO   *XLink, XML Base, XPath, XSLT*

XSL

The Extensible Stylesheet Language (XSL) creates style sheets specifically for XML pages. It is based on XML itself and has two primary parts: a language for transforming XML documents and a vocabulary for formatting XML-structured documents. XSL style sheets control the presentation of your XML information, by converting the original XML document into an HTML or other document format using the formatting controls specified in the XSL language.

The XSL Transformations (XSLT) specification became a World Wide Web Consortium (W3C) recommendation in November 1999. This recommendation defines the syntax and semantics used in converting XML documents into other document formats. The second portion of the specification, XSL Formatting (XSL-FO), provides a series of formatting objects and properties to be applied to the XML classes within your document, controlling the document's appearance when rendered.

NOTE   *Read more on the XSL specifications at* http://www.w3.org/Style/
            XSL/.

Cascading Style Sheets only work with the objects and elements predefined in your XML document. XSL surpasses that by adding content, displaying attributes, and converting your document format to HTML. XSL even has the ability to sort through your data so that only select portions are displayed.

XSL Features

XSL has these primary features above and beyond what CSS provides:

- Paging and Scrolling. XSL incorporates an advanced paging and scrolling system allowing you to have the same control over formatting of both scrollable and page-based documents. Keep in mind that XSL does not support the finite control over object placement available with desktop publishing products, but does improve on the page-formatting controls available with CSS.

- Selectors and Tree Construction. XSL includes improved formatting commands, which support specific patterns of selectors and the application of formatting options to those selectors.

- Extended Page Layout Model. XSL supports controls for identifying the exact dimensions of a page or frame and controlling how each individual segment of XML data will be placed within those pages.

- An Area Model. XSL allows developers to control the spacing of blocks, lines, objects, and specific areas of pages by extending the properties available. The XSL area model allows you to describe the relationship and adjust the spacing between individual letters, words, lines, and blocks of information.

- Internationalization and Writing Modes. XSL surpasses CSS by allowing text to flow from top to bottom as well as left to right and right to left.

- Linking Controls. XSL can specifically format the text of a link, as well as the objects, lines, words, or letters that follow a link. In addition, you can alter the content of the links target to control the placement of the target text upon your screen, or the manner in which the link's target is displayed in relation to the link itself.

CSS and XSL Compared

There is quite a lot that CSS cannot do, or can do only with difficulty, that XSL excels at:

- CSS cannot change the order of appearance of document content. XSL can.

- CSS cannot display attribute values, only use them as selectors. XSL can both display attribute values and use them as selectors.

- CSS doesn't address the need for formatting printed or printable documents. XSL provides finite control of printed pages through its page model controls.

SEE ALSO *Cascading Style Sheets, Style Sheets, XSL-FO, XSLT*

XSL-FO

XSL-FO is the formatting aspect of XSL. XSL-FO style sheets cannot be linked directly to an XML document because the XSL-FO vocabulary styles its own document's content, not another document's. XSL-FO content comes from one of two sources: an XSLT style sheet transferred to it from a source XML document or as literal text from the XSLT style sheet's templates. You will rarely work with an XSL-FO style sheet as a standalone, static document. Instead, its structure and content are included as the output of an XSLT style sheet.

The XSL-FO specification defines a large number of elements and attributes describing a set of containers for content. Each container is represented in XSL-FO code using a selection of attributes/properties. Within XSL-FO formatting statements are objects, representing text sequences, images, and tables, to name a few. XSL-FO provides a vocabulary complex enough to offer a complete range of complex layouts. XSL-FO's vocabulary represents nothing but presentation, making it sort of an enhanced version of CSS.

XSL-FO Example

Take for a moment this example document:

```
<?xml version="1.0"?>

<?xml-stylesheet type="text/xsl" href="orders.xsl"?>

<order>

    <customer> R. Cypher </customer>

    <ordertotal> 103.99 </ordertotal>

</order>
```

Using this simple order document that contains only a customer name and the order total amount, we could use XSLT to transform the document to XSL-FO instead of HTML. All of the elements prefixed with xsl: belong to the XSL Transformations language, whereas all the elements prefaced with the fo: prefix are part of the XSL-FO specification

```
<xsl:stylesheet version="1.0"

    xmlns:xsl="http://www.w3.org/1999/XSL/Transform"

    xmlns:fo="http://www.w3.org/1999/XSL/Format">

  <!-- Template rule to stop default text
  processing -->

  <xsl:template match="text()"/>

  <!-- Template rule for processing order element -->

  <xsl:template match="order">

    <fo:root xmlns:fo="http://www.w3.org/1999/XSL/
    Format">

      <fo:layout-master-set>

        <fo:simple-page-master page-master-
        name="main"
```

195

```
                margin-top="72pt" margin-
                bottom="72pt"

                margin-left="72pt" margin-
                right="72pt">

                <fo:region-body margin-
                bottom="72pt"/>

         </fo:simple-page-master>

      </fo:layout-master-set>

      <fo:page-sequence>

         <fo:sequence-specification>

            <fo:sequence-specifier-alternating

                page-master-first="main"
                page-master-odd="main"

                page-master-even="main"/>

         </fo:sequence-specification>

         <fo:flow flow-name="xsl-region-body">

            <fo:block font-size="24pt"
            line-height="27pt"

                      font-weight="bold">

               <xsl:value-of select="customer"/>

            </fo:block>

            <fo:block font-size="18pt" line-
            height="21pt"

                      font-weight="bold">

               Total: $<xsl:value-of
               select="ordertotal"/>

            </fo:block>

         </fo:flow>

      </fo:page-sequence>

   </fo:root>

   </xsl:template>

</xsl:stylesheet>
```

This style sheet contains a single functional template rule manipulating the document's root order element. Once transformed, you get this XSL-FO style sheet containing just the formatting elements, and the text from the original XML document:

```
<fo:root xmlns:fo="http://www.w3.org/1999/XSL/
Format">

    <fo:layout-master-set>

        <fo:simple-page-master page-master-
           name="main"

           margin-top="72pt" margin-bottom="72pt"

           margin-left="72pt" margin-
             right="72pt">

             <fo:region-body margin-bottom="72pt"/>

        </fo:simple-page-master>

    </fo:layout-master-set>

    <fo:page-sequence>

        <fo:sequence-specification>

            <fo:sequence-specifier-alternating

                page-master-first="main" page-
                master-odd="main" page-master-
                even="main"/>

        </fo:sequence-specification>

        <fo:flow flow-name="xsl-region-body">

            <fo:block font-size="24pt" line-
            height="27pt" font-weight="bold">

                R. Cypher

            </fo:block>

            <fo:block font-size="18pt" line-
            height="21pt" font-weight="bold">

                Total:$103.99

            </fo:block>

        </fo:flow>

    </fo:page-sequence>
```

```
</fo:root>
```

XSL-FO Software

There are three reasons that there aren't very many XSL-FO development programs available:

1. The XSL-FO standard itself has not yet been finalized.

2. The XSL-FO standard is large and complex, containing hundreds of elements and attributes that must be supported by software.

3. There has been very little pressure from potential developers.

The few software products available for XSL-FO can be classified as either native XSL-FO renderers or converters from XSL formatting objects to Adobe PDF format. Links to the most stable XSL-FO renderers are found at the W3C Web site at *http://www.w3.org.*

XSL-FO Renderers

A native XSL-FO renderer interprets formatting commands in order to display the document content in a predefined way. With few programs being able to display native XSL-FO-formatted content, there are more documents being converted into PDF files than XSL-FO files.

Turning Objects into PDF Files

The majority of effort spent on developing XSL-FO software has been spent on converting XSL-FO documents into Adobe PDF format. Adobe's free, downloadable, cross-platform Acrobat Reader program makes this an attractive option, providing users of these programs with the confidence that the resulting documents will be able to be viewed and printed exactly as desired by whomever needs to see them.

XSLT

The easiest way to make XML presentable is to turn it into something that can be formatted easily and read by a hundred easily accessible programs, such as a Web page, a print catalog, or a SMIL presentation.

An XSLT style sheet completes a document transformation using a series of one or more template rules. An XSLT processor performs the desired transformation(s) on the XML source document, transferring the results into an output file or directly onto a document viewer. XSLT is the only completed XSL specification, and it is enjoying support Internet Explorer 5.5.

Linking an XSLT to an XML Document

To link an XSLT style sheet to your XML document, use the <?xml-stylesheet?> processing instruction shown below:

```
<?xml-stylesheet type="text/xsl" href="uri"?>
```

SEE ALSO *<?xml-stylesheet?>, Processing Instructions, Style Sheets*

XSLT Example

To use XSLT to transform a simple order document into an HTML document, you use a series of <xsl:template> elements and match statements to collect the data from specific elements, and then write them to the HTML output. Take for a moment this example XML document:

```
<?xml version="1.0"?>

<?xml-stylesheet type="text/xsl" href="orders.xsl"?>

<order>

    <customer> R. Cypher </customer>

    <ordertotal> 103.99 </ordertotal>

</order>
```

To translate this into an HTML document, only displaying the customer name and order total, you would perform the following transformation:

```
<xsl:stylesheet version="1.0"

      xmlns:xsl="http://www.w3.org/1999/XSL/Transform"

      xmlns="http://www.w3.org/TR/REC-html40">


    <xsl:template match="text()"/>


    <xsl:template match="order">

        <html>

            <head><title>Order Information
            </title></head>

            <body>

                    <h1><xsl:value-of
                    select="customer"/></h1>
```

```
          <h2>Total: $<xsl:value-of
          select="ordertotal"/></h2>

       </body>

   </html>

   </xsl:template>

</xsl:stylesheet>
```

Be aware that an XSLT style sheet must be a well-formed XML document itself, including not only the XSLT code but also the other document instructions, HTML in this case.

The result of passing this style sheet through an XSLT processor, given the above XML document, will be the following HTML document:

```
<html>

  <head>

    <title>Order Information</title>

  </head>

  <body>

    <h1>R. Cypher</h1>

    <h2>Total:$103.99</h2>

  </body>

</html>
```